Glenn P. Anderson
NDTS
4/19/67
Review Copy

God
Meets Us Where
We Are

An Interpretation

God of Brother Lawrence

Meets Us Where
We Are

HAROLD WILEY FREER

𝄐

ABINGDON PRESS • nashville and new york

To my wife, Dorothy, known to many as Dot (whose interruptions have slowed down the production of this work and whose love has touched every page of it), not for anything she does or has done, but just because she is she and love is love —and that is that!

Preface

God meets us where we are. We need not "climb the heavenly steeps" to find him in some distant place. He comes to us in the routine of our daily living, just as he came to Israel in biblical times. In the first book of the Bible, Genesis 11:5, we read that when men in their arrogance decided to build a tower with its top in the heavens, "the Lord came down to see the city and the tower, which the sons of men had built." In the last book of the Bible, Revelation 1:1, we find that when God wished to reveal to his servants coming things, "he made it known by sending his angel to his servant John." In between these two incidents are hundreds of similar instances. To us too, in the intensity of the emotional experiences that touch us, in our joy and in our sorrow, in our hope and in our despair, in our humility and in our pride, in our loving and in our hating, in our friendships and in our loneliness, he reveals himself. Only we are not aware of him.

The secret of prayer is this awareness of his constant presence. Prayer opens our minds and hearts to a sense of his presence. He "speaks" to us in the events of each day, and our response to him is our prayer. Such a response is a growing process that moves from kindergarten through adolescence into a maturing devotion.

In Brother Lawrence we can see this maturing devotion reaching its height. For three hundred years his practice of the presence of God has been available to us. Either we have not known of this man and his message, or we have treated him lightly as one who found God's presence in an age far more simple than ours. Yet he calls our complex, sophisticated generation to a maturing faith that recognizes a living truth: God does meet us where we are.

A simple, farm lad who became the cook in a monastery, Brother Lawrence practiced the presence of God with a realism that is disturbing to our God-is-dead indifference of today. We stand in judgment before this man, for he found for himself and his friends, and for us today, a way of constant awareness that leads into a maturing faith. His finding may well be put into a single sentence, which he wrote in his Third Letter: "Were I a preacher, I should, above all other things, preach *the practice of the Presence of God;* and were I a 'director,' I should advise all the world to do it, so necessary do I think it, and so easy too."

This book is to help us discover ourselves and our devotion in the light of the experience of Brother Lawrence. We will look at the man and his message first, seeing just what he meant by his pregnant phrase "practicing the Presence of God." Then we will examine the twelve practices by which in part he came to know continually this presence, taking time ourselves to experiment with these. Finally, we will consider certain basic ideas which underlie these practices, ideas which in turn should call us to a maturing faith.

He lived in a forbidding century, the seventeenth. He himself shared for a time in the Thirty Years' War, a religious war that ravaged the continent. In England one king was beheaded, and another one deposed. In America settlers were hugging the seaboard precariously as they fought Indians and disease. Times indeed were foul. Yet he discovered in the vicissitudes of life that God met him where he was. What he found in the midst of so much violence and poverty I believe we may find in our generation with its violence and poverty.

Each chapter is introduced by appropriate scriptural passages, followed by selected quotations from the writings of Brother Lawrence. These latter are marked for ease of reference by "C" or "L" for Conversations or Letters, and include the paragraphs and pages from the complete text given in the Appendix.

HAROLD WILEY FREER

Acknowledgments

I am very grateful to the editors of Forward Movement Publications, 412 Sycamore Street, Cincinnati, Ohio, for permission to use their edition of "Brother Lawrence: His Letters and Conversations on the Practice of the Presence of God." The entire text is found in the appendix of this volume. This edition is by far the finest translation of Brother Lawrence, giving sixteen instead of the usual fifteen letters and offering dates for the writing of many of these. This text may also be purchased in pamphlet form from Forward Movement Publications at a nominal sum by those who may wish extra copies.

I would like to express my appreciation also to the publishers who have granted permission for the various quotations throughout this book. These are noted individually in the footnotes.

Contents

PART ONE

THE MAN AND HIS MESSAGE

Introduction

"The world is used to receiving an endless number of books at the hands of clerkly and learned men—soon to forget or reject most of them as no great loss.

"But it has a way of treasuring a certain Fisherman's memories taken down by a bright young companion; or the fortunes of a wayfarer grubbed out on paper by a Tinker twelve years in jail. Peter's *Gospel* and Bunyan's *Pilgrim's Progress* are secure as long as men shall read. And so perhaps is this present little book. Men have been reading it for their good ever since its humble author died just two hundred and fifty years ago.

"There must have been something rare in a monastery cook that a Grand Vicar should listen to his talk and go home and make notes of it; and that high-placed persons should beg of him not the recipe for a sauce but his secret of a happy life. This secret, sharp critics may say, is not the whole of wisdom, not a complete system either of philosophy or theology. But even today it is a life-saver to the harried citizen pulled one way by mystery and the other way by matter-of-fact. Your average man will stop and listen to a cook who knows God, when the animadversions of theologians and philosophers only weary him as babblings in a strange tongue.

"Brother Lawrence lived in times strangely like our own. He

began life as Nicholas Herman in Lorraine—at one of the many alternations when the province was French. In his boyhood began that Thirty Years' War which drew all Europe into its bloody maw—and still has some part in the outraged world of 1941.

"No doubt Nicholas Herman was one of millions sucked into that vortex, for first he was a common soldier. Later, he himself tells us 'that he had been a footman to Monsieur Fieubert, the treasurer, and that he was a great awkward fellow, who broke everything.'

"There are all too many of us now past middle age who feel soiled and weary—the bloom rubbed off from our aspirations— our hopes scaled down to the living of a life more mediocre every day. To such it comes like second wind to consort with a man of fifty who takes hold of himself and finds heaven on earth among the pots and pans of an institution's kitchen. We may demur that he was of finer stuff than we; but No, he pleads, I did nothing but let God have His own way with me." [1]

---

[1] From the Foreword by Gilbert P. Symons of "Brother Lawrence: His Conversations and Letters on the Practice of the Presence of God."

1

A Cook
as Spiritual Director

And when Jesus finished these sayings, the crowds were astonished at his teaching, for he taught them as one who had authority, and not as their scribes. (Matt. 7:28-29.)

That which was from the beginning, which we have heard, which we have seen with our eyes, which we have looked upon and touched with our hands, concerning the word of life . . . that which we have seen and heard we proclaim also to you, so that you may have fellowship with us; and our fellowship is with the Father and with his Son Jesus Christ. (I John 1:1, 3.)

Since you desire so earnestly that I should communicate to you the method by which I arrived at that **habitual sense of God's Presence,** *which our Lord, of his mercy, has been pleased to vouchsafe to me, I must tell you that it is with great difficulty that I am prevailed on by your importunities; and now I do it only upon the terms that you show my letter to nobody. If I knew that you would let it be seen, all the desire that I have for your perfection would not be able to determine me to it. (1L, 1, p. 191.)*[1]

That if this was my design, viz., sincerely to serve God, I might come to him (Brother Lawrence) as often as I pleased, without

---

[1] "L" represents one of the sixteen Letters, "C" one of the four Conversations, the paragraph and page as noted.

*any fear of being troublesome; but if not, that I ought no more to
visit him. (1C, 10, p. 182.)*

When the chief deputy of a cardinal seeks out a monastery
cook as his spiritual counselor, two qualities of true greatness
are revealed. One is the humility of a high ecclesiastical dig-
nitary who is willing to learn from a menial lay brother. The
other is the simplicity of an amateur who, without embarrass-
ment of things religious, speaks of what he has found.

How often an amateur is able to teach a professional. Brother
Lawrence did. On August 3, 1666, M. Beaufort, Grand Vicar
of Cardinal de Noailles, his chief deputy and administrative
assistant, went to the monastery of the Order of the Carmelites
Dechausses in Paris to interview the cook. Here he found
Brother Lawrence, a lay brother, whose simple statement of his
practice of the presence of God so moved the Grand Vicar that
he hastened home to write down his conversation. A second
visit in September, another in November, then a fourth in
November, 1667, completed the four conversations which have
come down to us. After the death of Brother Lawrence in 1691,
the four conversations along with sixteen letters written by the
cook, mostly to nuns, were gathered together, and a year later
the little book that we now have was first printed.

Who was this cook, "who in the midst of the most exacting
occupations, has learnt so well to accord action with contemplation, that for the space of more than forty years he hardly ever
turned from the Presence of God"? [2]

Brother Lawrence was born as Nicholas Herman in 1611, the
son of peasants in Lorraine, at that time a French province.
During his boyhood the Thirty Years' War began, and Herman
became a soldier. Though in later life he never mentioned his
soldiering, he did write in his Eighth Letter as though he knew
the work of a soldier. To a woman who sought advice about a

---

[2] From the Preface to the original French edition, 1692.

wounded soldier, Brother Lawrence suggested he pray often:
"A little remembrance of God, one act of inward worship,
though upon a march and sword in hand, are prayers which,
however short, are nevertheless very acceptable to God; and far
from lessening a soldier's courage in occasions of danger, they
best serve to fortify it. . . . It is very fit and most necessary for a
soldier, who is daily in danger of his life, and often of his
salvation" (8L, 2, 3, p. 200).

Tradition gives us two tales from his war years. One is that
he was captured by German forces and was accused of spying.
Though he denied he was a spy, his indifference when he was
told that he was to be executed so took the enemy by surprise
that they released him. The other tale says he was wounded in
the leg, not in battle but ignominiously by a stray cannonball
rolling from its storage place. We know he did have a crippled
leg, for he told M. Beaufort that "he was lame and could not
go about the boat but by rolling himself over the casks" (2C, 8,
p. 183).

After his term of soldiering, he became footman to M. Fieubert, the treasurer. Even though "he was a great awkward
fellow who broke everything," he was brought into the house
occasionally to serve as assistant to the butler, but his clumsy
fingers and awkward manner soon put an end to this.

Then it was that he decided to enter the monastery. As he
told M. Beaufort, he thought that "he would there be made to
smart for his awkwardness and the faults he should commit,
and so he should sacrifice to God his life, with its pleasures; but
that God had disappointed him, he having met with nothing but
satisfaction in that state" (1C, 4, p. 181). How sensitive he
was to his clumsiness and how mistakenly he believed God
would punish him for nature's blunder in giving him so ungainly
a body. Rather, he was satisfied with that state.

Even as a youth Nicholas Herman was deeply religious.
When he was eighteen, God "had done him a singular favor" in
bringing about his conversion. It was exceedingly simple. "That

in the winter, seeing a tree stripped of its leaves, and considering that within a little time the leaves would be renewed, and
after that the flowers and the fruit appear, he received a high
view of the providence and power of God, which has never
since been effaced from his soul." (1C, 2, p. 181.)

How like Jeremiah's was that conversion, as we shall see in
more detail in Chapter 7. Both the prophet and the young farm
lad knew the power and beauty of nature, and each, through a
tree, was brought to a realization of the greatness of God. (Cf.
Jer. 1:11-12.) Though Jeremiah often argued with God and
threatened at times to leave his prophesying, he never quite
could turn from the inward compulsion of God's spirit. (Cf.
especially Jer. 20:7-18.) Herman left no word concerning argument. Instead, as Brother Lawrence, he told the Grand Vicar
that his high view of God "had perfectly set him loose from the
world, and kindled in him such a love for God that he could
not tell whether it had increased during the more than forty
years he had lived since" (1C, 2, p. 181). Later, he also told
M. Beaufort that "he had long been troubled in mind from a
sure belief that he was lost; that all the men in the world could
not have persuaded him to the contrary; but that he had thus
reasoned with himself about it: *I engaged in a religious life
only for the love of God, and I have endeavored to act only for
Him; whatever becomes of me, whether I be lost or saved, I
will always continue to act purely for the love of God. I shall
have this good at least, that till death I shall have done all that
is in me to love Him*" (2C, 2, pp. 182-83).

With that high view of God behind him and with no sense
of purpose within him apart from God, he entered the monastery and assumed the name of Brother Lawrence. It was soon
after 1640, when he was about thirty years of age.[3]

---

[3] In a letter written in June, 1682, he wrote about himself: "You must
know that during the forty years and more that he had spent in religion"
(2L, 2, p. 192). In another letter written in 1689 to a mother superior, he
said, "You and I have lived a monastic life more than forty years" (10L, 2,
p. 201).

At the time of M. Beaufort's second visit in September, 1666, Brother Lawrence told him about his work in the kitchen, adding that "he had found everything easy during the fifteen years that he had been employed there" (2C, 9, p. 184). Evidently, upon admission to the monastery as a lay brother, he had served at least ten years in the stables and on the farm before his promotion to cook.

Also, during his cooking tenure, he had been sent into Auvergne, then into Burgundy, to buy wine for the monastery. He declared he had no turn for business, just as later he was to state that he had a great aversion to serving in the kitchen; but because he had accepted obedience to his superior, so that he could rightfully say to God: *"It was His business he was about,"* he had found both buying trips and cooking chores "very well performed." In 1666, after more than twenty-five years in the monastery, fifteen as a cook, "he was very well pleased with the post he was now in; but that he was as ready to quit that as the former, since he was always finding pleasure in every condition by doing little things for the love of God" (2C, 10, p. 184).

How much longer he served as cook we do not know. The four interviews by M. Beaufort, along with letters passed to others by recipients against his will (he told a mother superior he hesitated to write her, but did "only upon the terms that you show my letter to nobody"), brought unusual attention to this lay brother. Yet we know nothing more about his outward state, except that ill health in his latter years bothered him. Yet hardly "bothered" him in our modern usage of the term. For he wrote, "I have been often near expiring, but I never was so much satisfied as then. Accordingly, I did not pray for any relief, but I prayed for strength to suffer with courage, humility, and love" (15L, 1, p. 206). Difficult though it was in the beginning to arrive at this state of mind, as he further told his friend, he believed he must act always "purely in faith." So, in his last letter, written to the same friend, he wrote: "If we knew how much He loves us, we should always be ready to receive equally and with indifference from His hand the sweet and the bitter" (16L, 1, p. 206).

Within a week after writing this counsel, he died. It was mid-February of 1691, when he was eighty years of age. He was buried in the churchyard of the monastery, but men could not forget him. The four conversations and his scattered letters were quickly put together in a small volume and later was reprinted in many editions.

An ordinary lay brother, a large-boned, awkward fellow straight from the farm and soldiering and work in the stable, found in the kitchen and in wine-buying trips for his monastery an acute sense of the presence of God. So profound and yet so simple was this sense of presence that men from his day until now have searched in his writings for his secret. An ordinary man, because of his complete surrender to God, had become an extraordinary one.

2
The Heart
of His Message

Rejoice always, pray constantly, give thanks in all circumstances; for this is the will of God in Christ Jesus for you. (I Thess. 5:16-18.)

> Thou dost show me the path of life;
>   in thy presence there is fullness of joy,
>   in thy right hand are pleasures for evermore. (Ps. 16:11.)

> When my soul was embittered,
>   when I was pricked in heart,
> I was stupid and ignorant,
>   I was like a beast toward thee.
> Nevertheless I am continually with thee;
>   thou dost hold my right hand. (Ps. 73:21-23.)

For we are the temple of the living God; as God said,
>   "I will live in them and move among them,
>   and I will be their God;
>   and they shall be my people." (II Cor. 6:16.)

*I make it my only business to persevere in His holy Presence, wherein I keep myself by a simple attention and an absorbing passionate regard to God, which **I may call an actual Presence of God;** or, to speak better, a silent and secret conversation of the soul with God. (6L, 10, p. 198.)*

*That we should establish in ourselves a sense of God's Presence
by continually conversing with Him. (1C, 5, p. 181.)*

Brother Lawrence lived in a monastery. We do not. Is it
possible for us, in the midst of busy activity, thrust into the
world, to find the sense of presence that he discovered? I believe
it is. How we may do this we will examine rather carefully
in Part Two. There we will look at twelve practices whereby
we may open ourselves to God's grace, from which, as we
respond, should come the deepening sense of his presence. First,
though, let us see just what Brother Lawrence meant by that
phrase.

In utter simplicity he states it: "a silent and secret conversation of the soul with God." Deep within himself he knew the
indwelling God. Together they—his spirit and the spirit of the
living God—communed. Not by word of mouth, not even by
thought, but within the hidden reaches of his inner being,
Brother Lawrence conversed with God. He was one with God,
just as Jesus prayed that all who followed him later would be
"even as thou, Father, art in me, and I in thee, that they also
may be in us" (John 17:21).

This experience began, though, in simple thinking of God.
When asked by a member of his Society how this habitual
sense of God had come, "he told him that, since his first coming
to the monastery, he had considered God as the *end* of all his
thoughts and desires, as the mark to which they should tend
and in which they should terminate.

"That in the beginning of his novitiate he spent the hours
appointed for private prayer in thinking of God, so as to convince his mind of, and to impress deeply upon his heart, the
Divine existence, rather by devout sentiments, and submission
to the lights of faith, than by studied reasonings and elaborate
meditations" (4C, 17-18, p. 189).

He was no philosopher, no trained theologian to rationalize

his awareness of God. He just *knew* God was there, with a
heart-awareness, and with that God he carried on his continual
conversation.

He did not permit anything to interfere with that conversation. Whatever might come between him and God was to be
discarded. Whatever might lead him away from God was to
be renounced. "All consists *in one hearty renunciation* of everything which does not lead us to God in order that we may
accustom ourselves to a continual conversation with Him, with
freedom and in simplicity. That we need only to recognize God
intimately present with us, and to address ourselves to Him
every moment, that we may beg His assistance for knowing
His will in things doubtful, and for rightly performing those
which we plainly see He requires of us; offering them to Him
before we do them, and giving Him thanks when we have done.

"That in this conversation with God we are also employed in
praising, adoring, and loving Him unceasingly, for His infinite
goodness and perfection." (4C, 2-3, p. 187.)

Yet this is no conversation with God in a private monastery
cell. Brother Lawrence's entire day, regardless of the nature
of his work, was filled with such a "silent and secret conversation." Away from the monastery to buy wine, "he said to God
It was His business he was about, and that afterwards he
found it very well performed" (2C, 8, p. 183).

When he fulfilled his duties in the monastery itself, it was
the same. "So, likewise, in his business in the kitchen (to which
he had naturally a great aversion), having accustomed himself
to do everything there for the love of God, and with prayer,
upon all occasions, for His grace to do his work well, he had
found everything easy during the fifteen years that he had
been employed there." (2C, 9, p. 184.)

Of course he would have conversed with God had his wine-
buying been to his liking, or his cooking a natural pleasure.
Anyone can talk intimately with God in times of joy and delight.
Yet he had no business sense, he declared; nor did he like

kitchen work, in spite of his fifteen years of employment. Here is the true test of one's sense of God's presence—to know it when doing what one normally would not choose to do.

Further, so habitual did this sense of presence become to him that Brother Lawrence said that he "was more united to God in his ordinary occupations than when he left them for devotion in retirement, from which he knew himself to issue with much dryness of spirit" (3C, 7, p. 186). Here is no person withdrawn from life, living sentimentally on the mountaintop of pious "spirituality." Rather, like some of us who have found "dryness of spirit" in regular services of worship, or even in our times of personal devotion, he found this sense of presence in his regular and usual work. Hence, he never complained that duties called him from his devotion, that he could find no time to be apart with God.

Brother Lawrence would have understood Jane Merchant, when she wrote,

> Today, I need to go
> Down to my secret place
> Where shadowed waters flow
> Beneath the gentle grace
> Of willows. I have need
> To feel the waters cool
> Upon my brow and to feed
> On silence of the pool.
> But urgent duties fill
> My day, and I must find
> My comfort in the still
> Pool pictured in my mind.[1]

Jane Merchant is a cripple, confined to a bed. Yet she learned like Brother Lawrence to find God's presence in the midst of her duties.

[1] "Still Pool." Reprinted from *Christian Home*, October, 1953. Copyright 1953 by Pierce and Washabaugh.

The same experience was that of de Caussade who wrote two hundred years ago of Jesus, Mary, and Joseph: "We are not told that these holy persons sought out holy things and circumstances, but only holiness in their circumstances." [2]

De Caussade revealed the same temperament of Jane Merchant and Brother Lawrence. In one's duties one will find holiness, that sense of oneness with God. For him this is to be found in two ways: "in accomplishing the duties imposed on us by the general laws of God and the Church, and by the particular state of life which we have embraced"; and "in the loving acceptance of all that God sends us every moment." [3]

This is the essence of Brother Lawrence's message. Whatever duty he faced, at the whim or direction of his superiors, he gladly fulfilled it to the best of his ability. After all, it was his duty to serve God. Hence, he did not search out "holy things and circumstances." He found holiness in all circumstances.

[2] J. P. de Caussade, *Self-Abandonment to Divine Providence* (London: Burns & Oates, 1959), p. 16.
[3] *Ibid.*, p. 5.

3

The Constancy
of His Presence

Whither shall I go from thy Spirit?
  Or whither shall I flee from thy presence?
If I ascend to heaven, thou art there!
  If I make by bed in Sheol, thou art there!
If I take the wings of the morning
  and dwell in the uttermost parts of the sea,
even there thy hand shall lead me,
  and thy right hand shall hold me.
If I say, "Let only darkness cover me,
  and the light about me be night,"
even the darkness is not dark to thee,
  the night is bright as the day;
  for darkness is as light with thee. (Ps. 139:7-12.)

  Even though I walk through the
    valley of the shadow of death,
    I fear no evil;
  for thou art with me. (Ps. 23:4.)

*That we need only to recognize God intimately present with us,
and to address ourselves to Him every moment. (4C, 2, p. 187.)*

Joan laughed. "What a funny thing we're doing!" she said.
Seated on the floor in the corner of the living room, surrounded

by other boys and girls of her youth group, she waited the beginning of a service of worship.

"What's funny about it?" the leader asked.

"It's Friday night, and we're not in church," she replied. "This is no place or time for worship!"

Sixteen teen-agers had shared a picnic supper as the introduction to their weekend retreat. Now they had come together for their first session. Dressed in slacks and jeans, and sprawled over chairs or cushions spread on the floor, they quieted down for the opening service of worship. Then it was that Joan laughed.

Worship belonged to church. It also belonged to Sunday—especially eleven o'clock Sunday morning, or for the youth group, and perhaps seven in the evening too. But Friday! And in the living room of a home!

Young Jacob thought the same thing. He deceived his father Isaac and cheated his brother Esau. Afraid of his brother's wrath, Jacob fled toward Haran, his mother's home. There he would find refuge, a job, even a wife.

That first night in the wilderness Jacob had a dream of angels ascending and descending a ladder to heaven. On awakening, Jacob said, " 'Surely the Lord is in this place, and I did not know it.' And he was afraid, and said, 'How awesome is this place! This is none other than the house of God, and this is the gate of heaven' " (Gen. 28:16-17).

God was not supposed to be there. God belonged to the family altar at home, the sacred place of ritual and ceremony. Yet on a journey, while fleeing from the wrath of a brother, while looking for a refuge, a job, a wife, Jacob met God. No wonder he was afraid of that awesome spot. The Lord God was there! God had escaped from the imprisonment of man's superstition, and Jacob did not know what to do with that encounter.

Nor do we. As long as we can keep God imprisoned in church or creed or book, or keep him bound to a definite time schedule, we can handle him. Let him escape from that special time or place, and we are afraid. He may interfere with our business or pleasure; he must not be permitted "to run loose." We are like the Grand Inquisitor of Dostoevsky's *The Brothers Karamazov,* disturbed by the coming again of the Christ to sixteenth-century Spain: "Is it Thou? Thou? . . . What canst Thou say, indeed? I know too well what Thou wouldst say. And Thou hast no right to add anything to what Thou hadst said of old. Why, then, art Thou come to hinder us? For Thou hast come to hinder us, and Thou knowest that."

Today we do not mind so much his coming again, just so it is the right place and hour. Then we are not taken by surprise with his entrance into our daily life. Then he does not hinder us. That is why we build for him an enclosed place. No wonder R. Buckminster Fuller declares: "The church, once the largest and busiest of community structures, now exists only as a memorial to the necessity of a special building for God." [1]

For Brother Lawrence there was no special time or place. He found God in intimate fellowship at all times and in the most unlikely places. In the sanctuary, yes, but in the kitchen also, or while traveling to buy wine for the monastery. Aware of God's presence, Brother Lawrence "addressed" him at every moment. It was the constancy of that presence that surprised men in his time as well as in our own. He did not "seek" God in the sanctuary, or in the quiet of his own cell. Rather, he was "found" by God in every place and at every hour. God is the great searcher. "The time of business . . . does not with me differ from the time of prayer, and in the noise and clatter of my kitchen, while several persons are at the same time calling for different things, I possess God in as great tranquillity as if I were upon my knees at the Blessed Sacrament." (4C, 24, p. 190.)

---

[1] See *No More Secondhand God* (Carbondale: Southern Illinois University Press, 1962).

If today we expect to find God only in a church building, only during a service of worship, only in a quiet time, only in what we may foolishly call a "religious" experience, then probably we will not "find" him at all. It is wrong to believe that only in certain emotionally filled "mountaintop" experiences will we realize his presence. Remember how Simon Peter in his ignorance ("not knowing what he said," Luke 9:33) wanted to build three booths on the mount of transfiguration?

It is the same with our prayers. If, while we are in the sanctuary on bended knee, or at work with mind and hands busy, or in the quiet of our own inner closet, or standing before a window open to God's world, or lying on a sick bed, we lift our hearts in simple prayer, knowing that God is there, then it is quite likely that we know his presence at every other time. If, on the other hand, we seldom have that sense of presence, we may be sure that our prayers will often feel too heavy to rise even to the ceiling.

God does not reveal himself normally in the unusual. He reveals himself in the daily round of our living. Martin Buber, the great Jewish scholar, said: "The signs of address are not something extraordinary, something that steps out of the order of things, they are just what goes on time and again, just what goes on in any case." Hence, we are aware of God at nearly every moment, or we are not actually aware of him at all. God is in the midst of us, if we ascend to heaven or if we make our bed in Sheol or if we take the wings of the morning and dwell in the uttermost parts of the sea.

Zephine Humphrey found this to be true in the most humble of household tasks, the emptying of the garbage:

Among all the moods of the spirit, that of simple awareness is the most precious. The divine condition cannot be induced; but it can be wooed and waited on with a humble mind. Readiness and expectation can become the habits of the heart. As I stand, with

the lid of the garbage pail in one hand and my empty tin dish in
the other, something arrests me. I look up wonderingly. Then—oh,
beauty and sweetness of the summer day! serenity and detachment
of the summer world! I am invaded, flooded by it, caught away
into it, dazzled by its exceeding loveliness. Before me the orchard
lies peaceful and green, with birds in its widely branching old
trees, crickets and butterflies in its grass, blue sky above it and
golden sunshine irradiating it. Beside me is the glowing garden,
and beyond are the untroubled hills. . . . Could we, if we tried, be
aware more frequently? [2]

Ken thinks so. Brought out of filth and drunkenness through
the companionship of Alcoholics Anonymous, he says simply:
"God meets us where we are. For each step we take toward
God, he will take two toward us. He becomes a part of us, and
we of him. God walks with us, not ahead pulling, nor behind
pushing. There is no compulsion. He is in the lowest dens of
iniquity as well as the most elaborate cathedrals. He is where
he is needed and wanted."

God does meet us where we are. This is the essence of Christian love, of *agape* love, that we need not "climb the heavenly
steeps to bring the Lord Christ down." He is already here.
When the angel told this truth to the shepherds, "the glory of
the Lord shone round them, and they were filled with fear"
(Luke 2:9). We today need not be afraid. We know that this
is the Lord's expected action.

Again Martin Buber wrote:

One eats in holiness, tastes the taste of food in holiness, and
the table becomes an altar. One works in holiness, and he raises
up the divine sparks which hide themselves in all tools. One
walks in holiness across the fields, and the soft songs of all
herbs, which they voice to God, enter into the song of our soul.

[2] Quoted in Winfred Rhoades, *To Know God Better* (New York: Harper
& Brothers, 1958), p. 71.

One drinks in holiness to each other with one's companions, and it is as if they read together in the Torah. One dances the roundelay in holiness, and a brightness shines over the gathering. A husband is united with his wife in holiness, and the Shekinah rests over them.[3]

[3] From *Hasidism* (New York: The Philosophical Library, 1948), p. 32.

4

The Glory
of the Lord

When Moses entered the tent, the pillar of cloud would descend and stand at the door of the tent, and the Lord would speak with Moses. And when all the people saw the pillar of cloud standing at the door of the tent, all the people would rise up and worship, every man at his tent door. Thus the Lord used to speak to Moses face to face, as a man speaks to his friend. (Exod. 33:9-11.)

Moses said, "I pray thee, show me thy glory." And he said, "I will make all my goodness pass before you, and will proclaim before you my name 'The Lord'; and I will be gracious to whom I will be gracious, and will show mercy on whom I will show mercy. But," he said, "you cannot see my face; for man shall not see me and live." And the Lord said, "Behold, there is a place by me where you shall stand upon the rock; and while my glory passes by I will put you in a cleft of the rock, and I will cover you with my hand, until I have passed by; then I will take away my hand, and you shall see my back; but my face shall not be seen." (Exod. 33:18-23.)

And the Word became flesh and dwelt among us, full of grace and truth; we have beheld his glory, glory as of the only Son from the Father. (John 1:14.)

For it is the God who said, "Let light shine out of darkness," who has shone in our hearts to give the light of the knowledge of the glory of God in the face of Christ. (II Cor. 4:6.)

No man has ever seen God; if we love one another, God abides in us and his love is perfected in us. (I John 4:12.)

*And I make it my only business to persevere in His holy Presence, wherein I keep myself by a simple attention and an absorbing passionate regard to God, which I may call an **actual Presence of God**; or, to speak better, a silent and secret conversation of the soul with God. (6L, 10, p. 198.)*

There is not in the world a kind of life more sweet and delightful than that of a continual walk with God. Those only can comprehend it who practise and experience it. (3L, 3, p. 194.)

*I must, in a little time, go to God. What comforts me in this life is that I now see Him by **faith**; and I see Him in such a manner as might make me say sometimes, **I believe no more, but I see**. I feel what faith teaches us, and in that assurance and that practice of faith I will live and die with Him. (12L, 6, p. 204.)*

The Hebrews believed in a living God who revealed his presence in the concrete experiences of daily life. He was no abstraction to be defined in set phrases, neatly tied in semantics. Not until the New Testament do we find definitions for God, and then only three simple ones in the writings of John with its Hellenistic influence. These three—"God is spirit" (John 4:24), "God is light" (I John 1:5), and "God is love" (I John 4:8)—still show the Hebrew background of the author. For God appears in no vacuum, no event isolated from human experience. Rather, John says that in Jesus we "behold his glory."

In the early Old Testament stories God is very much physically present. He walks in the garden "in the cool of the day." He comes down to watch the building of the Tower of Babel like any sidewalk superintendent. He appears to Moses in a burning bush that was not consumed. In the wilderness journey he comes to speak to Moses as a man to his friend in the pillar of cloud that settled at the door of the tent of meeting. When the people recognized the presence of God in the cloud, they stood to worship, every man in front of his own tent.

Yet even Moses was unable to see God face to face. That
was too much for mortal eye. He was God's friend, though, so
Moses stood in the cleft of a rock, his eyes covered by the
hand of God while his "glory" passed by. Then God lifted his
hand, that Moses might see his back. But man could not see
God's face—and live.

Wherever and whenever this glory appeared, it was always
a manifestation of deity in the natural world, the only world
the Hebrews knew. In time such experiences received the name
of "Shekinah," or "the dwelling," from the Hebrew root, "to
dwell." In the Shekinah God dwelt with his people for a time,
revealing to them his presence. Later on, the Hebrews turned
from their anthropomorphic ideas of God, until by New Testament times God no longer was "pictured" as a man. Yet the
word "glory" continued to be the symbol of God's presence.
John Baillie points out that both in the later years of the Old
Testament and in the New Testament "glory" often is only
another word for "presence."

Upon the shepherds on Christmas morn "the glory of the
Lord shone around them" (Luke 2:9). At Cana of Galilee
Jesus did the first of his signs "and manifested his glory" (John
2:11). At the tomb of Lazarus, Jesus chided Martha, "Did
I not tell you that if you would believe you would see the glory
of God?" (John 11:40). The martyred Stephen looked up and
"saw the glory of God" (Acts 7:55). In the New Jerusalem
there will be no need of sun or moon, "for the glory of God
is its light" (Rev. 21:23). Best of all, and at the heart of the
Christian faith, is Paul's affirmation of the presence in Jesus,
"the glory of God in the face of Christ" (II Cor. 4:6).

It is this sense of the presence of God, the Shekinah of his
glory in these and other biblical references, as well as the continuing sense of presence in our time, that has led John Baillie
to write: "We have to do, not with an absent God about whom
we have a certain amount of information, but with a God whose

living and active presence with us can be perceived by faith in a large variety of human contexts and situations." [1]

Such an eye of faith Brother Lawrence had. In his kitchen work, on his knees to receive the Blessed Sacrament, during his journeys to buy wine for the monastery, when picking up a straw from the floor, he persisted in a "silent and secret conversation of the soul with God." He *knew* he was in "His holy Presence," an "actual Presence of God." This is the statement of faith of a simple lay brother, untrained in philosophy and theology. Yet one so trained, John H. Hick, has written:

Behind the world—to use an almost inevitable spatial metaphor—there is apprehended to be an omnipotent, personal Will, whose purpose toward mankind guarantees men's highest good and blessedness. The believer finds that he is at all times in the presence of this holy Will. . . .

Thus the primary religious perception, or basic act of religious interpretation, is not to be described as either a reasoned conclusion or an unreasoned hunch that there is a God. It is, putatively, an apprehension of the divine presence within the believer's human experience. It is not an inference to a general truth, but a "divine-human encounter," mediated meeting with the living God.[2]

Brother Lawrence believed such a meeting was taking place every moment of his day. He could converse with God and did, with praise, with thanksgiving, with desire, "the commerce of love." During the stated times of corporate prayer under the monastery rule, in his own periods of private devotion, in all his free moments when there was nothing else to call him, he constantly talked with God. "The time of business . . . does not with me differ from the time of prayer, and in the noise and clatter of my kitchen, while several persons are at the same time calling for different things, I possess God in as great tranquillity

---

[1] *The Sense of the Presence of God* (New York: Charles Scribner's Sons, 1962), p. 261.

[2] See *Faith and Knowledge* (2nd ed.; Ithaca: Cornell University Press, 1957), p. 129. Quoted in *The Sense of the Presence of God*, p. 259.

as if I were upon my knees at the Blessed Sacrament." (4C, 24, p. 190.)

Then too, he knew the "sweet and delightful" joy of "a continual walk with God." Like the disciples on the way to Emmaus whose hearts burned within as the risen Christ talked with them, Brother Lawrence knew that another walked with him through the day. True enough, as he said, "Those only can comprehend it who practise and experience it." Yet it is a living experience for many of us. One such, a teacher and farmer's wife, wrote:

On the porch alone after supper, I had been reading and meditating. It had been a showery evening, and several times I walked to the east end of the porch to watch a brilliant rainbow form and fade, then reform to fade again against a sky of brightest blue.

In my devotions my attention was drawn to a prayer by Gerald Heard: "O eternal light, radiate us away, that we being emptied of everything but Thee, Thy presence may be manifest in all and through all." Such overpowering feelings were welling up within me, I thought I must "walk this off."

I turned down the paths which lead to the back fields of our farm. As I walked, I looked up to see great billowing clouds, rolling and racing across the sky, too beautiful to behold, and I was forced to look away. But then the trees took on a vividness of color, as did the fields, and every blade of grass. Where *could* I look? God's blinding radiance was everywhere and in every thing.

When I turned to retrace my steps, I was facing the huge, blazing, setting sun and God was in that more than in anything else. I could not look at the sun as I was filled with the knowledge that we cannot look at God in his unveiled glory. As He was filling all around me, so He was filling me. In those moments or minutes, He was everything and I was nothing.

But this was very painful and I cried as I stumbled along, "O God, why do you do this to me? I cannot stand it!"—so overwhelming and overpowering was His Presence.

I returned to the house and the porch, and there came to understand and to articulate something of that which had just happened to me. The Psalmist described his experience thusly, "All thy waves and thy billows are gone over me." Like St. Augustine, "I shall never ask for greater certainty of God, only for more steadfastness in Him."

I know not why He came to me through the beauty of that summery evening. But I know He came. He comes no more often than He does, I am sure, because we would not be able to take it. I know not why He came, but I know He came, and humbly I thank Him.

Did she really *see* all this? She did and in the way of Brother Lawrence. "What comforts me in this life is that now I see Him by *faith;* and I see Him in such a manner as might make me say sometimes, *I believe no more, but I see.*" (12L, 6, p. 204.)

Brother Lawrence did "see" God, as the teacher did, but not with the physical eye. Each saw as alone we can "see" God, with the eye of faith. Yet the Exodus verse still holds true: "man shall not see me and live." For both of them died, died to self, to self-love, to self-desire. They were born anew. So James Reid wrote:

God had acted creatively. . . . The coming of God's light . . . is the action of God, and its effect is creative. A new thing has happened. The soul has been born. To realize this truth and identify our experience with the light of God's glory in the face of Jesus Christ will bring in us the recognition of God's presence in our life and set us exploring and discovering the love of Christ.[3]

[3] *The Interpreter's Bible* (Nashville: Abingdon Press, 1953), X, 317.

5

Every Day
Is His Day

"Now is my soul troubled. And what shall I say, 'Father, save me from this hour'? No, for this purpose I have come to this hour. Father, glorify thy name." Then a voice came from heaven, "I have glorified it, and I will glorify it again." (John 12:27-28.)

Then the righteous will answer him, "Lord, when did we see thee hungry and feed thee, or thirsty and give thee drink? And when did we see thee a stranger and welcome thee, or naked and clothe thee? And when did we see thee sick or in prison and visit thee?" And the King will answer them, "Truly, I say to you, as you did it to one of the least of these my brethren, you did it to me." (Matt. 25:37-40.)

That the most excellent method he had found of going to God was that of **doing our common business** *without any view of pleasing men, and (as far as we are capable)* **purely for the love of God.** *(4C, 7, p. 187.)*

That he was more united to God in his ordinary occupations than when he left them for devotion in retirement, from which he knew himself to issue with much dryness of spirit. (3C, 7, p. 186.)

That he had no qualms; for, said he, when I **fail in my duty,** *I readily acknowledge it, saying,* **I am used to do so; I shall never do otherwise if I am left to myself.** *If I fail not, then*

I give God thanks, acknowledging that the strength comes from Him. (2C, 20, p. 185.)

I do not say that therefore we must put any violent constraint upon ourselves. No, we must serve God in a holy freedom; we must do our business faithfully, without trouble or disquiet, recalling our mind to God meekly, and with tranquillity, as often as we find it wandering from Him. (4L, 4, p. 195.)

That in his trouble of mind he had consulted nobody, but knowing only by the light of faith that God was present, he contended himself with directing all his actions to Him, i.e. doing them with a desire to please Him, let what would come of it. (2C, 13, p. 184.)

A prayer class, studying the discipline of generosity as a means toward deepening communion with God, faced certain practices. Two of these raised serious question: (1) Consider giving him a whole day of your time. Give it, and (2) Give him yourself—and renew the gift, over and over, until it becomes a reality.

A puzzled young mother asked: "How can this be done, with the care of the children and the running of the household? I just can't take out the time. We must be real in this."

Others agreed. This we must do, give ourselves in full commitment to God. This is true generosity. When, though, can we do this? Not when children are at home, not when household chores fill our day, not when we must share in Girl Scouts and Cub Scouts and PTA, to say nothing of church school and the woman's society. Perhaps twenty years from now, when the children are all away and time becomes heavy on our hands. Until then, we must be "real."

One of the group interrupted. "But we *do* give him a day of our time. I give him every day of my life. So do you. We call ourselves Christians. That doesn't mean to me that I go to church Sunday and give myself to him between eleven and twelve. If that's all I give him, I haven't given him anything.

I give him all my day, and every day. This is my Christian commitment. Oh, I know I hold back much of some days. I want my way in them, or I am not loving in them. But I try. It isn't his fault that I make such a mess of it. I do offer myself to him in every day and for every day. I *do* give myself to him the whole day. I believe that is what we must do if we are to be disciplined Christians. I am with him every day. We all are!"

"What do you mean?" the group wanted to know.

"Well, I am doing each day what I think God wants me to do —getting the family off to work and school, making the beds, cleaning house, visiting my neighbor. These things are part of my job. I don't understand all of God's will for me, but I do believe these household chores are a significant part of it. Then when I come to prayer class, or attend a woman's society's meeting, or go to church service, I'm still doing what I think he wants me to do.

"I know I make many mistakes, because my self, that old ego of mine, keeps getting in the way. But I'm trying. I'm offering him every bit of my day. My quiet time and my busy work are all the same, only different ways of being with him through the day. He doesn't want just my periods of devotion or specific "church" services like helping with the bazaar or teaching church school. He wants all my time."

This answer is similar to what I have already been pointing out, that God's presence is not to be found *only* in services of worship or in places of worship, or even on certain holy days, and surely not *only* in times of so-called acts of Christian social concern. He is in all our days, the totality of them, each and every one of the twenty-four hours.

How did the prayer class member come to this answer? First, do what you believe God wants you to do, even though it is different from all others. "For this purpose I have come to this hour," Jesus said when the Greeks came seeking him (John 12:27). "Doing our common business . . . for the love of God," said Brother Lawrence. According to our present state

in life, whether one is a housewife, another a politician, a third
a businessman, still another a craftsman, we are to do the work
we are called to in the best way possible. It is as Paul wrote:
"God has appointed in the church first apostles, second prophets,
third teachers, then workers of miracles, then healers, helpers,
administrators, speakers in various kinds of tongues." (I Cor.
12:28.) Each is to fulfill his calling with his finest workmanship. Anything else would be a denial of our calling before God.

Second, do your work, then let it go, without anxiety of its
success or failure. Watch a TV western for relaxation. If the
leisure rested you, let it go without any sense of guilt in "wasting" your time. Lead the woman's society's program. Let it go
without asking everyone, "Did I do all right?" or without
whipping yourself by saying, "I should have done better." If
you could have done better, you were a poor workman, not
doing his will. If you did the best you could with what you had,
then he was pleased with what you offered. Forget it, let it go,
and wait quietly for your next opportunity, whether it is making
a cake for a sick neighbor, or leading a discussion group, or
selling a car, or offering a prayer of thanksgiving, or mending
the water faucet, or receiving the Holy Sacrament. As Brother
Lawrence said, "Do our business faithfully, without trouble
or disquiet."

Third, be what you are, using what you have. The seminary
student wishing to be a little "Fosdick" or a little "Billy
Graham" merely brings laughter upon himself. God called one
Harry Emerson Fosdick, one Billy Graham, but many Toms,
Dicks, and Marys into the pulpit. Each is to give in his own way
just what he has, and no more. When he gives all he has, God
makes more of it. In Marc Connelly's play, *Green Pastures,*
de Lawd called Noah to build an ark and so save mankind.
After arguing that he was not worthy of so great a task, Noah
finally spoke the truth as he accepted it: "I ain't very much,
but I'se all I'se got." It is this that God wants from us. Only
in our conceit and pride do we imitate others' binding ourselves

to unsuitable taskmasters. We are to be free men and women, free to be ourselves, free to be children of a compassionate God who sees what we are and rejoices in our free use of what we have. To two men, one with five talents, the other with only two, Jesus said the same thing after each had used just what he had, "Well done, good and faithful servant; you have been faithful over a little, I will set you over much; enter into the joy of your master" (Matt: 25:23).

Fourth, accept lovingly each day as it comes, with all that it brings. It is this, according to de Caussade, that helps bring holiness into every day: "accepting what most frequently cannot be escaped, and suffering with love, *i.e.* with consolation and sweetness, what is too often endured with weariness and disgust." Not liking kitchen work ("to which he had naturally a great aversion") nor the "very unwelcome task to him" of buying wine for the monastery, Brother Lawrence yet said to God, "It was His business he was about." Naturally the work turned out well! No wonder, then, that he could write further: "Be satisfied with the state in which God places you."

This is the way to a lasting joy, a peace that does abide. This makes every day his day. He asks not for an occasional day, a day set apart for him; he asks for all our days. "Therefore, my brothers, I implore you by God's mercy to offer your very selves to him: a living sacrifice, dedicated and fit for his acceptance, the worship offered by mind and heart." (Rom. 12:1 NEB.)

6

Breaking Down
the Partition

Behold, the days are coming, says the Lord, when I will make a new covenant with the house of Israel and the house of Judah, not like the covenant which I made with their fathers when I took them by the hand to bring them out of the land of Egypt, my covenant which they broke, though I was their husband, says the Lord. But this is the covenant which I will make with the house of Israel after those days, says the Lord: I will put my law within them, and I will write it upon their hearts; and I will be their God, and they shall be my people. And no longer shall each man teach his neighbor, and each his brother, saying, "Know the Lord," for they shall all know me, from the least of them to the greatest, says the Lord; for I will forgive their iniquity, and I will remember their sin no more. (Jer. 31:31-34.)

So, whether you eat or drink, or whatever you do, do all to the glory of God. (I Cor. 10:31.)

Then I saw a new heaven and a new earth; for the first heaven and the first earth had passed away, and the sea was no more. And I saw the holy city, new Jerusalem, coming down out of heaven from God, prepared as a bride adorned for her husband; and I heard a great voice from the throne saying, "Behold, the dwelling of God is with men. He will dwell with them, and they shall be his people, and God himself will be with them. . . ."

And I saw no temple in the city, for its temple is the Lord God the Almighty and the Lamb. And the city has no need of sun or moon to shine upon it, for the glory of God is its light, and its lamp is the Lamb. (Rev. 21:1-3, 22-23.)

*So, likewise, in his business in the kitchen (to which he had natural-
ly a great aversion), having accustomed himself to do everything
there for the love of God, and with prayer, upon all occasions, for
His grace to do his work well, he had found everything easy
during the fifteeen years that he had been employed there. (2C,
9, p. 184.)*

*Accustom yourself, then, by degrees thus to worship Him, to beg
His grace, to offer Him your heart from time to time in the midst
of your business, even every moment, if you can. Do not scrupulously confine yourself to fixed rules, or particular forms of devotion, but act with faith in God, with love and humility. (5L, 3,
p. 196.)*

*If sometimes he is a little too much absent from the **Divine
Presence**, which happens often when he is most engaged in his
outward business, God presently makes Himself felt in his soul
to recall him. He answers with exact fidelity to these inward
drawings, either by an elevation of his heart toward God, or by a
meek and loving regard to Him; or by such words as love forms
upon these occasions, as for instance, **My God, behold me,
wholly thine: Lord, make me according to Thy heart.** And
then it seems to him (as in effect he feels it) that this God of love,
satisfied with such few words, reposes again, and rests in the depth
and center of his soul. The experience of these things gives him
such an assurance that God is always deep within his soul, that no
doubt of it can arise, whatever may betide. (2L, 4, pp. 192-93.)*

To a woman complaining because difficult home problems
upset her love for God, Evelyn Underhill wrote: "Knock down
the partition between the living room and oratory, even if it
does mean tobacco smoke and incense get a bit mixed up." She
refused to let her friend place her everyday living and her
Christian faith in separate compartments.

How often we try to keep them apart—things "secular" on
one hand, things "religious" on the other. Members of a beginning prayer class agreed to have a time of quiet each day for

personal devotions. One woman found in this quiet time a source of strength and tranquillity for the entire day. In one class session, though, she fussed angrily that a neighbor came in nearly every day and interrupted her quiet time. "What am I to do with her?" she asked in frustration.

"Tell her to go home, that you're having your quiet time," I told her.

"Why!" she exclaimed in horror. "I couldn't do that!"

"That is just what you *are* doing," I told her. "Not by actual words, perhaps, yet by tone of voice, and certainly by inner thoughts."

So the woman asked herself two questions. First, is my neighbor a busybody or a lonely person, seeking friendship? Why does she come to me? What can I offer her? Second, what good is my quiet time if it is only for myself and cannot include my neighbor? Can I truly love God if I do not love my neighbor too? Is it possible for me to keep them separate?

Ecclesiastes writes that there is a time for everything, a time to seek and a time to lose, a time to be quiet and a time to speak. Charles M. Schulz, creator of the cartoon strip, "Peanuts," raises a question about this, but lets his reader choose the answer. He describes a ball game in which Lucy plays in center-field. A ball is hit to her and falls at her feet. Charlie Brown runs out to ask why she didn't catch it, for all she needed to do was to put out her glove. Her reply is brief, "I was having my quiet time."

Lucy's piety is very close to blasphemy. The ball game must not interfere with her religious practice. "Religion" for her must come first. It is used as an escape from responsibility. So it was with the woman keeping her religion separate from her home problems. The partition must be knocked down, her counselor wrote.

This is not to say that there is no need for the oratory. Of course this must have its place. Yet Brother Lawrence went beyond most of us. "To be with God, there is no need to be continually in church. We may make an oratory of our heart wherein to retire from time to time to converse with Him in meekness, humility, and love." (5L, 2, p. 196.)

Most of us, in order to pray, withdraw from our normal busyness. We think God is to be found only when we stop all action. Then, afterwards, we may continue our duties. Brother Lawrence suggests the right way for us. "Accustom yourself, then, by degrees thus to worship Him, to beg His grace, to offer Him your heart from time to time in the midst of your business, even every moment, if you can." (5L, 3, p. 196.)

This same thought was in the mind of C. S. Lewis, when he wrote his friend:

There is danger in the very concept of *religion*. It carries the suggestion that this is one more department of life, an extra department added to the economic, the social, the intellectual, the recreational, and all the rest. But that whose claims are infinite can have no standing as a department. Either it is an illusion or else our whole life falls under it. We have no non-religious activities; only religious and irreligious.

Religion, nevertheless, appears to exist as a department, and, in some ages, to thrive as such. It thrives partly because there exists in many people a "love of religious observances," which I think Simone Weil is quite right in regarding as a merely natural taste. . . . This department of life, labelled "sacred," can become an end in itself; an idol that hides both God and my neighbours. . . . I read in a religious paper, "Nothing is more important than to teach children to use the sign of the cross." Nothing? Not compassion, nor veracity, nor justice? *Voilà l'ennemi.*[1]

Was it a writer with the same kind of thinking who placed an advertisement in the religious press, seeking a curate for his parish, and ending with a phrase: "No surplice work except on Sundays"?

---

[1] *Letters to Malcolm: Chiefly on Prayer* (New York: Harcourt, Brace & World, 1964), pp. 30-31. Used by permission of Harcourt, Brace & World and Geoffrey Bles, Ltd.

Bruno James writes the truth. "We cannot expect to be recollected when we are on our knees if we ignore God all the rest of the day." [2] For we are, indeed, when we pray, what really we are when we do not pray. The two cannot be separated. Sam Jones, noted evangelist of a century ago, knew this only too well. Knowing himself and the divisions within himself, he warned: "Do what I say and not what I do."

With Brother Lawrence the two were the same. Again I quote from the Preface to the Original French Edition: "All, whatever their life-work, will find profit, for they will see herein a brother, busied as they are in outward affairs, who in the midst of the most exacting occupations, has learnt so well to accord action with contemplation, that for the space of more than forty years he hardly ever turned from the Presence of God."

[2] *Seeking God* (New York: Harper & Brothers, 1960), p. 47.

PART TWO

TWELVE PRACTICES OPENING THE HEART TO GOD'S GRACE

Introduction

These twelve practices of Brother Lawrence reveal to us ways by which we may open ourselves to God's grace. Not one of them in itself is able to assure us of a sense of his presence. If any of us by our own action were able to achieve this sense, we would have God at our command. We do not have him at our command. He is God, and we are the creatures of God. He alone is sovereign. He alone can command.

Yet in our "silent and secret conversation with God" we learn to become passive, to listen, and in that listening we hear him speak. The more we hear him speak, the more certain we are of his presence. "Then it is that abiding in His Holy Presence, we may continue our commerce of love, now by an act of adoration, of praise, or of desire; now by an act of sacrifice or of thanksgiving, and in all the manners which our mind can devise." (4L, 5, p. 195.)

So, in the words of Bruno Scott James, as we persevere through prayer,

Christ is gradually formed in us by the grace of God. And increasingly we become more and more passive as God works in us by love, and with both hands now freed of creatures we cling to him ever more closely. Finally there comes the stage in which more or less strongly we are conscious of God's presence within us. We can do nothing to acquire this sense (I use the word "sense" for want of a better, but in fact it is beyond the senses) and very little indeed to control it. At first it comes and goes, each time perhaps staying a little longer and growing a little stronger, until there come moments when it is so strong that the soul seems powerless to resist it and becomes, under its influence to an ever-increasing degree, unconscious of its surroundings and powerless to move; and at such times there is also the sense that it is no longer we who pray but Christ within us adoring his Father.

Whatever the occasion, this condition may become so strong, so irresistibly powerful, that anything can turn us toward God: a note in music, a beautiful view, the sight of some holy person, the chance word of a friend. . . . Here I must repeat once more that this sense of the presence of God within us, whether it be strong or weak, continuous or only occasional, cannot be acquired by any efforts of our own and it would be a great mistake to attempt to do so. It is an effect of Charity, a gift of the Holy Ghost, and it often seems to be given with little regard to the merits of the receiver.[1]

Nevertheless, we must do our share. Not without reason did Paul write, "Work out your own salvation with fear and trembling; for God is at work in you, both to will and to work for his good pleasure" (Phil. 2:12-13). Hence, these twelve practices offer us today similar ways to work out our own salvation, though with great fear and trembling, for after all it is God who works in us.

[1] *Seeking God,* pp. 41-42, 43.

7

Conversion

This word from the Eternal came to me: "Jeremiah, what do you see?" I said, "The shoot of a wake-tree." The Eternal said to me, "You have seen right; for I am wakeful over my word, to carry it out." (Jer. 1:11-12 Moffatt.)

In those days Jesus came from Nazareth of Galilee and was baptized by John in the Jordan. And when he came up out of the water, immediately he saw the heavens open and the Spirit descending upon him like a dove; and a voice came from heaven, "Thou art my beloved Son; with thee I am well pleased."

The Spirit immediately drove him out into the wilderness. And he was in the wilderness forty days, tempted by Satan; and he was with the wild beasts; and the angels ministered to him.

Now after John was arrested, Jesus came into Galilee, preaching the gospel of God, and saying, "The time is fulfilled, and the kingdom of God is at hand; repent, and believe in the gospel." (Mark 1:9-15.)

Now as he journeyed he approached Damascus, and suddenly a light from heaven flashed about him. And he fell to the ground and heard a voice saying to him, "Saul, Saul, why do you persecute me?" And he said, "Who are you, Lord?" And he said, "I am Jesus, whom you are persecuting; but rise and enter the city, and you will be told what you are to do." . . . Saul arose from the ground; and when his eyes were open, he could see nothing; so they led him by the hand and brought him into Damascus. . . . So Ananias . . . laying his hands on him . . . said, "Brother Saul, the Lord Jesus who appeared to you on the road by which you came, has sent me that you may regain

your sight and be filled with the Holy Spirit." And immediately something like scales fell from his eyes and he regained his sight. Then he
rose and was baptized. (Acts 9:3-8, 17-19.)

*He told me that God had done him a singular favor, in his conver-
sion at the age of eighteen.*

*That in the winter, seeing a tree stripped of its leaves, and consid-
ering that within a little time the leaves would be renewed, and after
that the flowers and fruit appear, he received a high view of the
providence and power of God, which has never since been defaced
from his soul. That this view had perfectly set him loose from the
world, and kindled in him such a love for God that he could not
tell whether it had increased during the more than forty years he
had lived since. (1C, 1-2, p. 181.)*

In the middle of the winter, when most trees stand barren
against the dull Judean sky, the youthful Jeremiah suddenly
came upon an almond tree. Blooming almost as early as January,
the almond is called in the Hebrew *shaqed,* the wakeful. With
pun-play on words the Lord asked Jeremiah what he saw. "The
rod of a wakeful tree," he said. "Yes," the Lord said, "and I
am wakeful (Hebrew *shoqed*) to perform my word." With
this vision the young man began his long years of prophecy.

In the vision of a tree in the wintertime Brother Lawrence
too met God, who "had done him a singular favor, in his conversion at the age of eighteen." As we noted earlier in Chapter 1,
both young men were deeply moved by their visions; yet these
came through a common, ordinary experience of nature, a tree
stark against the wintry sky. For the farm lad in Lorraine as
for the priest's son in Anathoth, God revealed himself in what
each of them had seen many times before, a tree in winter.
Only this time they responded, one to begin a ministry as
prophet and statesman, the other to receive "a high view of the
providence and power of God" not to be "effaced from his
soul" for his remaining threescore years and more.

How did God first reveal his presence to you, so that you knew unmistakenly that it was he? Each person's experience is quite different from every other person. Few are like Paul's, dramatic lights and sounds that shook his very foundations. For most of us in the common experiences of our daily living God meets us where we are.

So it came to a lad on the afternoon of his high school commencement. Not having memorized his brief speech for the evening ceremony, he wandered restlessly from room to room on the second floor of his home. Suddenly he glanced at the date as shown on an undertaker's scripture calendar, and read under the numeral:

> Fear not, for I am with you,
>   be not dismayed, for I am your God;
> I will strengthen you, I will help you,
>   I will uphold you with my victorious right hand
>   (Isa. 41:10).

Immediately he became quiet and went into his bedroom, where within thirty minutes he memorized the talk. That evening he presented it flawlessly. For more than twenty years afterward, he returned to that text in any kind of difficulty, drawing strength and hope for the moment from its quiet and assurance. Never once did he doubt that God was with him in that experience. He continued the use of that text, handling it mentally much as one handles a talisman, until in the compulsion of his spiritual growth he found suddenly that he no longer needed it as a crutch.

One day a minister, who for some years had written weekly reviews for the book page of a metropolitan Sunday newspaper, received a copy of a book about which he had heard nothing. In the flipping of the pages as he scanned it, his life was changed. In a month's time his wife knew something had happened, and before long his friends recognized it. Within six months his

entire congregation was aware of a vast change in his entire
ministry. The casual ruffling of the pages of *The Choice Is Always Ours*[1] turned into a careful reading of the book, followed
by the study of all the books on prayer that he could find, some
two hundred and more, an almost inhuman saturation of mind
and spirit. Then with his congregation he began a lifelong
search through prayer classes, depth Bible study, discussion
groups. Out of that joint search with his people have come
several books, and finally, this one. That I am that minister
is beside the point; the significance of what happened is that
in the ordinary routine of one's work, as minister and book re-
viewer, I met God face to face.

A Quaker author, Sylvia Shaw Judson, has presented in a
book some thirty pictures, a few in color, with a brief sentence
or two about each. The end of a bench in a Quaker meeting
house, a Grecian vase, modern and classical paintings, a carving
by a Canadian Indian, a plastic linear construction are a few of
these, all there to "communicate a sense of affirmation, of
wonder, of trust." For, she writes, "I have wanted particularly
to find examples with a sense of 'divine ordinariness,' a delicate
balance between the outward and the inward, with freshness
and a serene wholeness and respect for all simple first-rate
things, which are for all times and all people."[2]

This is Brother Lawrence's conversion, and mine, and yours
—a sense of "divine ordinariness," God's breaking into the
normal routine of our day. So we learn with Brother Lawrence:
"We can do *little* things for God. I turn the cake that is frying
on the pan for love of Him, and that done, if there is nothing
else to call me, I prostrate myself in worship before Him, who
has given me grace to work; afterwards I rise happier than a
king. It is enough for me to pick up but a straw from the
ground for the love of God." (4C, 21, p. 189.)

[1] Dorothy B. Phillips, ed. (New York: Harper & Row, 1960).
[2] *The Quiet Eye: A Way of Looking at Pictures* (Chicago: Henry
Regnery Company, 1959), p. 1.

Experiments in Thought and Action

1. Write in your notebook brief descriptions of your "Conversion" experiences, when God broke "into the normal routine" of your day. At these times did you know that it was God meeting you where you were? When and how did you come to realize it was his action in your life?

2. Have you had a dramatic conversion that could be dated, such as Paul's on the Damascus Road? What change in your life came as a result of this?

3. Have you known a conversion experience less dramatic, from which no sudden change came as far as you could tell? What were the lasting effects of such experiences?

4. Is God continuing to meet you where you are, breaking into your daily life?

8

Join a Church Fellowship

They are planted in the house of the Lord,
They flourish in the courts of our God. (Ps. 92:13.)

After three days they found him in the temple, sitting among the teachers, listening to them and asking questions; and all who heard him were amazed at his understanding and his answers. (Luke 2:46-47.)

And he came to Nazareth, where he had been brought up; and he went to the synagogue, as his custom was, on the sabbath day. (Luke 4:16.)

That he had desired to be received into a monastery, thinking that he would there be made to smart for his awkwardness and the faults he should commit, and so he should sacrifice to God his life, with its pleasures; but that God had disappointed him, he having met with nothing but satisfaction in that state. (1C, 4, p. 181.)

Of course we are not required to enter a monastery nor even to join a religious group in order to receive a sense of his presence through grace. Yet here is a practice as valid today as it was in the days of Jesus or in the time of Brother Lawrence.

Jesus regularly attended the synagogue, the center of worship and study for the community. After the return from the Exile and perhaps during the stay in Babylon, when there was no temple, the Jews met in buildings in local areas that became the centers for worship, for the school, for the judicial court, for other community gatherings, and even at times for the lodging of overnight guests. No longer was it necessary for long pilgrimages to a holy place where sacrificial rites were performed for a tribe or nation. Each village had its own center. The synagogue became the heart of the Jewish faith and, in turn, became the pattern for the Christian church and the Islamic mosque. Everyone in his own local community could come with his neighbors for worship and study. Later, when the temple was rebuilt, only on holy days would crowds come on pilgrimage.

To the synagogue in Nazareth Jesus came as a boy, and there he went every sabbath for worship and study. At the feet of the local scribe he learned to read the Scriptures and share in corporate worship. His practice was habitual, so much so that after leaving Nazareth, he still visited the synagogue in whatever community he lived. He knew the value of regular, faithful attendance upon corporate worship.

Brother Lawrence as the son of devout parents was raised in his local church. Was it more to him, though, than a place for worship in the midst of turmoil? We must remember that the Thirty Years' War was a religious war, that the churches of his time fomented it. Yet we must not judge his day by the conscience of our day, even if seemingly there is little difference about the feeling of war. Nevertheless, Brother Lawrence knew that if he were to grow in the Christian life, he must seek a fellowship of committed Christians. So he was received into the Order of the Carmelites Dechausses as a lay brother and entered their monastery in Paris.

Here he shared the daily offices in which as a lay brother he too was required to perform. Here he worked at menial tasks in farm and stable during his early years, and at cooking which he disliked during his middle years. Here he became confidant of many and spiritual guide to an unknown number in his last years.

Yet none of this growing would have been possible for him

had he not become a part of a fellowship for disciplined worship, study, and service. He did not come and go as he pleased, attending divine services only when a noted preacher was sent on mission, praying only when he felt a need for something, working only when it was a job to his liking. He belonged to a fellowship. He accepted its discipline. He shared its work, enjoyed its companionship, grew under its encouragement, and through it all, "met with nothing but satisfaction in that state."

Many seemingly devout persons today, not members of any church fellowship, seek "spiritual refreshment" in retreats, schools of prayer, gatherings of the Camps Farthest Out, the Ashrams, the Disciplined Order of Christ, and like movements. Such folk are always welcome in those meetings. Yet, they turn their backs upon a local church. They say: "The women are interested only in bazaars, suppers, and other money-making projects. The men have no greater concern than the latest bowling or golf score. The preacher is not spiritual. I don't see why I should join a church like that. I get my religion in these spiritual meetings!" In other words, they feast occasionally, fast often.

When Phillips Brooks was a young seminarian, he attended a students' evening prayer meeting in which several of his classmates prayed with considerable unction. To his surprise, the next morning the same students had not prepared their Greek lessons. With scorn Brooks said, "The boiler was not connected with the engine."

These are the folk who pray with unction at an annual camp meeting, but refuse to bear the drudgery of week-after-week church fellowship. They forget their own backgrounds.

How many of my readers were raised in churches where everyone was a Mary, where the preacher was "spiritual"? Except for rare occasions in school days, the ministers of the churches I regularly attended in my growing years were hardly more than a cut above the average, if that. Nevertheless, in those churches, through devout men and women, ministers and lay folk of vision and love, I found all that helped me grow in understanding of God and his love. My seeking was shared by others; my finding brought rejoicing to others. What is more, when I have attended retreats and camp meetings and spiritual life conferences, I have found that the leadership nearly always rested in the hands of faithful churchmen. It is the church fellowship, with its fine heritage of hymns and prayers and Scriptures, with its study groups of varied kinds, with its opportunities for service in outreach of the community—local, national, and even international—that has nurtured me, just as it has most of us. Without the church, the institutional church with all its faults, the local unit, and the larger denomination, I never would have found even an inkling of the sense of presence that is mine.

In these days of world revolution, when the church hardly knows its mission and often with helpless frustration wonders what it should do next, a remnant is still alive. These are the folk who read the analyses of church failure, who listen carefully to the prophets of change, who experiment with new programs, who venture into Babylon, who offer themselves to the leadership of the Spirit as they seek to be Christians in a non-Christian society. With living faith in the reality of their mission, they can say with realism: "The church is dead; long live the church!"

Experiments in Thought and Action

1. Are you a faithful and loyal member of a Christian church? If not, what valid reasons do you hold for rejecting such membership? If you are a member, how has its fellowship nurtured your faith?
2. What is your idea of the mission of the church to the world today? How may you share creatively in this mission?

9

Obedience to Superiors

Behold, to obey is better than sacrifice,
and to hearken than the fat of rams. (I Sam. 15:22.)

Listen to advice and accept instruction,
that you may gain wisdom for the future. (Prov. 19:20.)

He was praying in a certain place, and when he ceased, one of his disciples said to him, "Lord, teach us to pray, as John taught his disciples." (Luke 11:1.)

For whatever was written in former days was written for your instruction, that by steadfastness and by the encouragement of the scriptures we might have hope. . . . I myself am satisfied about you, my brethren, that you yourselves are full of goodness, filled with all knowledge, and able to instruct one another. (Rom. 15:4, 14.)

Children, obey your parents in the Lord, for this is right. . . .
Slaves, be obedient to those who are your earthly masters, with fear and trembling, in singleness of heart, as to Christ. (Eph. 6:1, 5.)

I was not disobedient to the heavenly vision. (Acts 26:19.)

That he retired to pray, according to the directions of his Superior, but that he did not want such retirement, nor ask for it, because his greatest business did not divert him from God. (2C, 11, p. 184.)

*Being questioned by one of his own society (**to whom he was*** *obliged to open himself)* by what means he had attained such an habitual sense of God. (4C, 17, pp. 187-88.)

But when we are faithful to keep ourselves in His holy Presence, and set Him always before us, this not only hinders our offending Him and doing anything that may displease Him, at least wilfully, but it also begets in us a holy freedom, and, if I may so speak, a familiarity with God, wherewith we ask, and that successfully, the graces we stand in need of.* (1L, 4, p. 192.)

Protestants, on the whole, do not have "superiors" in the sense of the Catholic "religious," *i.e.* the professional. The lay brother as well as the monk, the lay sister as well as the nun, take vows of obedience to the superior. Throughout the Roman Catholic Church, within the various Orders as well as in the general priesthood, all "religious" are under the discipline of obedience, the highest superior of all being the Pope.

All Christians, though Catholic or Protestant, lay or clerical, must be obedient. To whom, though, or to what must we be obedient?

Certainly like Paul we must be obedient to the heavenly vision. That vision comes in a different form to each of us, to no two of us alike. So Thoreau wrote in *Walden:* "If a man does not keep pace with his companions, perhaps it is because he hears a different drummer." Yet there is real danger in following our own drummer, lest we move at too great a tangent from the narrow path of that vision.

At this point a spiritual director, a person of insight and training, a teacher whose experience is rooted in history as well as in current events, is needed. Brother Lawrence saw this in his own commitment. For his own growth, to fulfill the inner calling toward a continual sense of presence, he sought a monastery where under the discipline of obedience he might find "a holy freedom," an obedience to a way of life grounded

---

* Emphasis added.

in history. He had a heavenly vision, but he needed to know more clearly the path it required.

Some folk foolishly seek the path of holiness, this continual sense of presence, without any real sense of calling. Like the seed sown on shallow soil, their growth is quick for a time; but there is no inner drive, no sensation of purpose, to withstand the heat and the drought of a disciplined life. Not having this heavenly vision, this all-consuming purpose, they wilt under the sun of obedience.

Martha Graham, in accepting the Second Aspen Award in the summer of 1965, said:

People have asked me why I chose to be a dancer. I did not choose to be a dancer. I was chosen to be a dancer, and with that you live all your life. When any young student asks me, Do you think I should be a dancer? I always say, If you can ask that question, no! Only if there is just one way to make life vivid for yourself and for others should you embark upon such a career.[1]

When one is chosen, as Brother Lawrence was, then he will seek whatever help he can find along the way. Then he supplements the heavenly vision with hard work. He is obedient to whomever and whatever will bring him to his goal.

During my seminary years I was an intern in a large church as assistant to the minister, Dr. Edward Weeks Cross. Though I learned a little about preaching and a little about pastoral work and a little about program planning, as he spoke specifically about these from time to time, it was through his own careful discipline, his painstaking preparation of his pastoral prayers, his almost fanatical plotting out of the church bulletin that its neatness and its correct English should make it worthy of usage in God's house, his nurturing of his inner devotion, his planning of his schedule so that he never had time to waste, yet always had time to spare for the needs of anyone who

[1] *Saturday Review,* August 28, 1965, p. 54.

called upon him—it was through all these and more that I was guided along the path of my own "heavenly vision." Only as I was obedient, obedient outwardly in part to the direction of my minister, obedient inwardly in part to that divine calling which I knew, did I grow.

Through the Scriptures, through the saints ancient and modern, through the teachers in fields seemingly quite distant from the "religious" field (such as Martha Graham and modern interpretative dancing), we find as Protestants those "superiors" whom we must obey. This is not, of course, because of any special human talent, their personal authority of position or experience that they may possess. Rather, it is because they are God's agents, who set us upon the way, then help trim our sails to the winds of God. To disobey them is to disobey God. As Evelyn Underhill points out: "Not to obey God is really a vote of non-confidence in God."

A young minister asked how he might discipline his devotional life. He heard within himself the call of God to do this. Yet he declared emphatically, "I don't like discipline!" Hence, when at his request some simple suggestions were made, such as reading a chapter from the New Testament daily and along with this, a chapter from one of the great spiritual classics, he said he didn't think he would do it. His refusal to obey was actually a vote of nonconfidence in God, whose inner urging he rejected.

Early one Monday morning another young minister played a round of golf with the club professional. "I'd give anything," he declared, "to play like you!"

The pro said, "Come out at six tomorrow morning, and each morning this week."

"Oh no," he cried, "I couldn't do that!"

He had neither a heavenly vision nor the discipline of persistence, of courage, of insight to obey even a dream. He never became a good golfer.

Brother Lawrence did not play golf. He did, though, have a

heavenly vision, and in the discipline of obedience, he found his
holy freedom, a continual sense of the presence of God. No
wonder he could write: "There is not in the world a kind of life
more sweet and delightful than that of a continual walk with
God. Those only can comprehend it who practice and experience
it; yet I do not advise you to do it from that motive. It is not
pleasure which we ought to seek in this exercise; but let us do
it from the motive of love, and because God would have us so to
walk" (3L, 3, p. 194).

Experiments in Thought and Action

1. Were you, in any sense of the word, "chosen"? If so, how
   have you been obedient to this call?
2. From your own experience describe the value of obedience.
   To whom or to what were you (and are you) obedient? Why
   were you obedient?
3. Is there a "superior" to whom you may give obedience as
   you seek to grow in the life of the spirit? From whom or
   from what do you now accept guidance?

10

Set Times
of Prayer

These things I remember,
  as I pour out my soul:
how I went with the throng,
  and led them in procession to the house of God,
with glad shouts and songs of thanksgiving,
  a multitude keeping festival. (Ps. 42:4.)

Every day I call upon thee, O Lord;
  I spread out my hands to thee. (Ps. 88:9.)

When Daniel knew that the document had been signed, he went to his
house where he had windows in his upper chamber open toward Jerusalem; and he got down upon his knees three times a day and prayed
and gave thanks before his God, as he had done previously. (Dan. 6:10.)

And he told them a parable, to the effect that they ought always to
pray and not lose heart. (Luke 18:1.)

Pray constantly. (I Thess. 5:17.)

*That with him the **set** times of prayer were not different from
other times; that he retired to pray, according to the directions of
his Superior. (2C, 11, p. 184.)*

*As for my set hours of prayer, they are only a continuation of the
same exercise. Sometimes I consider myself there as a stone before
a carver, whereof he is to make a statue; presenting myself thus*

71

before God, I desire Him to form His perfect image in my soul,
and make me entirely like Himself. (6L, 12, p. 198.)

In accordance with the custom of most monasteries of the
time and especially those of the Order of Carmelites, the
canonical hours, seven periods of prayer beginning with matins
with lauds soon after midnight and concluding with complin
soon after nightfall, were the set times of prayer which Brother
Lawrence observed each day. Even as a lay brother he was
required, as we have seen earlier, to share these with the monks.
Today all major orders still must join in daily use of the
breviary, the prayers for the canonical hours.

These set times of prayer are the practice sessions in which
the fingers of the mind play over the keys of the spirit until
the player is one with the Muse. No prayers said over and over
again will automatically create communion between God and
man. Yet such communion is impossible without persistent
prayer, beginning where necessary with the simplest form of
vocal prayer, then passing through mental prayer, until finally
the peak of prayer, contemplation, is reached. Though this
comes to us only through the grace of God, we must fulfill our
part.

So a child is taught verbal prayer at bedtime, which in the
earliest years has no meaning to him at all. Soon, though, he
catches the feel of the prayer, especially when his teacher, a
parent usually, has a sense of reverence and wonder. To the
learned patter of prayer the child then adds his own phrasing,
to bless a neighbor, a pet, or even a loved object like a teddy
bear. As the child grows, he passes through various stages of
religious experience according to backgrounds of home and
school and community. Where there is training in the life of
prayer, the child comes to sense a personal relationship,
normally for the Protestant, with Jesus. He is the intimate,
friendly person, so unlike the abstract God often far distant

from many Protestant and Catholic homes. Though most people
never outgrow this adolescent worship of the man Jesus, some
do go beyond it to the Christ of God. Then like Brother
Lawrence they come into a sense of presence.

For the Protestant today, except for those rare few enclosed
in monasteries or attached to lay centers, set times of prayer
are the regular services of worship in the churches. Even if
these services actually were times of worship (which they are
not for most folk), all of us know these are not enough for us
to learn the practice of the presence. They must be supplemented by daily worship, our own private devotion. When the
two, corporate prayer and private prayer, are both practiced
faithfully, then the ground is laid for the grace of God to act
in our lives. For these two are the foundations of interior
prayer in which communion is possible.

In the monastery Brother Lawrence found both. Through
the years the founders and heads of the various Orders worked
out deliberate and set patterns of prayer by which men might
practice their devotion. Rather than limiting men's thinking,
these patterns safeguarded them from wandering and frivolous
petitions. Contrast the Communion Collect (also known as the
Collect for Purity), for example—"Almighty God, unto whom
all hearts are open, all desires known, and from whom no
secrets are hid: Cleanse the thoughts of our hearts by the in-
spiration of thy Holy Spirit, that we may perfectly love thee,
and worthily magnify thy holy name"—with the extemporary
(and perhaps apocryphal) prayer of the woman who said, "We
thank thee, O God, for this day, and all thou hast brought us,
even as Shakespeare said—no, I believe it was one of the
prophets . . ."!

Hence, those who prayed corporately worshiped with saints
from many generations, whose heritage in turn was passed on
to ours. Yet the monasteries also left a place for the intimacies
of personal devotion, in which each heart according to its own
attrait might open itself to God's leading. In the training ground

of both corporate and personal prayer men and women grew to be saints, those who knew "an actual presence of God."

The same is possible for us today without our becoming members of a monastery. In the services of worship of our church we find the corporate worship without which we are lonely indeed. Those who from time to time find that their church offers little more than form in worship know how lonely this can be. Yet Mrs. Scudder, cultured, well traveled, devoutly Christian, when an untrained minister with undisciplined faith came to be her preacher, said: "I get nothing whatever from his sermons or his prayers, but I'm not going to let him keep me from worship. Every Sunday some place in the service I know God's presence." After all, she shared with others who too longed for deeper awareness of God's presence, and through the hymns and Scriptures, if in no other way, she stepped into the living stream of worship.

For those who stay away from church altogether, saying they need no such experience of worship with others, that God speaks to them in their solitude, there is only one answer. God can do this, but if they listen carefully, they will hear him say in the words of John: "If any one says, 'I love God,' and hates his brother, he is a liar; for he who does not love his brother whom he has seen, cannot love God whom he has not seen" (I John 4:20). For is not the scorn and contempt and pride that keeps one from worshiping with others only another word for hate?

Our Christian faith is a social one. Rare are those individuals who are called to hermit-like existence. As C. S. Lewis writes: "It is well to have specifically holy places, and things, and days, for, without these focal points or reminders, the belief that all is holy and 'big with God' will soon dwindle into a mere sentiment." [1]

On the other hand, those who do attend corporate worship,

[1] *Letters to Malcolm,* p. 75.

but feel no need for private worship, are eating only one day in the week. Their spiritual life is anemic, starving for daily sustenance. There can be no growing in the life of prayer, no deepening consciousness of the presence of God, without "continually conversing with Him."

In the more than six thousand prayer classes using the curriculum of *Two or Three Together*,[2] each member has agreed to have a daily time of quiet, in which to pray for his fellow class members, for his church, for his family, for other persons and situations which God may place upon his heart. In time many have found that this time of quiet becomes a time of listening, when the inner heart is sensitive to God's leading.

So it was that Brother Lawrence considered himself there "as a stone before a carver, whereof he is to make a statue; presenting myself thus before God, I desire Him to form His perfect image in my soul, and make me entirely like Himself." In a similar picture de Caussade wrote:

Let the point of the knife and the needle work. Let the brush of the master cover you with a variety of colors which seem only to disfigure the canvas of your soul. Correspond with all these divine operations by the uniform and simple disposition of a complete self-abandonment, self-forgetfulness, and application to your duty. Keep to the line of your own advance and, without knowing the map of the country or the details, names and directions of land you are passing through, walk blindly along that line and everything will be indicated to you if you remain passive. Seek only the kingdom of God and his justice in love and obedience and all the rest will be given you. [3]

Of course, either attendance upon corporate worship or the regular practice of daily devotion, can be a mere form. This we know. "If these holy places, things, and days," writes C. S. Lewis, "cease to remind us, if they obliterate our awareness

---

[2] Harold W. Freer and Francis B. Hall, eds. (New York: Harper & Row, 1954.)

[3] *Self-Abandonment to Divine Providence*, p. 67.

that all ground is holy and every bush (could we but perceive it) a Burning Bush, then the hallows begin to do harm." [4] They need not do harm. They are to open us to God's action, so that we may see that every day is his day. "Then it is that abiding in His holy Presence, we may continue our commerce of love, now by an act of adoration, of praise, or of desire; now by an act of sacrifice or of thanksgiving, and in all manners which our mind can devise." (4L, 5, p. 195.)

Experiments in Thought and Action

1. Do you regularly attend the corporate services of worship of your church? Are these truly times of worship for you? What can you do to enrich these periods of corporate worship?
2. Do you have a time of daily personal devotion? If so, what do you do in it? In what way is it more than a form to practice?
3. Read a chapter a day from the New Testament, beginning with Matthew and continuing through Revelation. After completing the 260 chapters, repeat them, using a different New Testament translation.
4. Read also a chapter or section each day from one of the spiritual classics, such as Augustine's *Confessions*, Thomas à Kempis' *Imitation of Christ, Meister Eckhart,* and so forth.

[4] *Letters to Malcolm,* p. 100.

11

Confession
of Sin

And I said: "Woe is me! For I am lost; for I am a man of unclean lips, and I dwell in the midst of a people of unclean lips; for my eyes have seen the King, the Lord of hosts." (Isa. 6:5.)

Those who are well have no need of a physician, but those who are sick; I came not to call the righteous, but sinners. (Mark 2:17.)

And Jesus said to him, "Why do you call me good? No one is good but God alone." (Luke 18:19.)

If we confess our sins, he is faithful and just, and will forgive our sins and cleanse us from all unrighteousness. (I John 1:9.)

That he had placed his sins betwixt him and God, as it were to tell Him that he did not deserve His favors, but that God still continued to bestow them in abundance. (2C, 2, p. 183.)

That he was very sensible of his faults, but not discouraged by them; that he confessed them to God, but did not plead against Him to excuse them. When he had so done, he peaceably resumed his usual practice of love and adoration. (2C, 12, p. 184.)

That we ought without anxiety to expect the pardon of our sins from the blood of Jesus Christ, laboring simply to love Him with all our hearts. That God seemed to have granted the greatest favors to the greatest sinners, as more signal monuments of His mercy. (2C, 18, p. 185.)

*That he had no qualms; for, said he, when I **fail** in my duty, I readily acknowledge it, saying, **I am used to do so; I shall never do otherwise if I am left to myself.** If I fail not, then I give God thanks, acknowledging that the strength comes from Him. (2C, 20, p. 185.)*

I am filled with shame and confusion when I reflect, on one hand, upon the great favors which God has bestowed and is still bestowing upon me; and, on the other, upon the ill use I have made of them, and my small advancement in the way of perfection. (10L, 2, p. 201.)

With a profound personal insight that would do justice to one trained in modern psychology, Brother Lawrence accepted himself with all his limitations. He did not try to fool himself; hence, he raised no barriers between himself and others, nor between himself and God. "I am what I am," he seemed to say.

Along with this understanding of himself, though, went an equally profound sense of the greatness of God, "a high view of the providence and power of God" that began with his conversion and developed remarkably during his years as a cook. His frank and realistic acceptance of himself came in large part because of this high view of God. Yet, on the other hand, his high view of God came in part from the deepening awareness of himself. Each was necessary to the other. He who hides from himself hides from God, and he who hides from God hides from himself.

He did neither. He faced himself in truth, one of the most difficult experiences any man must endure; and he faced God in humility. Along with Moses, Brother Lawrence knew that he could not see God and live, live to himself, live in his old ways. He "saw" God, and died to himself; so that "I resolved to give myself up to God as the best satisfaction I could make for my sins, and for the love of Him to renounce all besides" (6L, 3, p. 197).

First of all, he did know himself, so that he could place his sins "betwixt him and God," recognizing that he did not deserve God's grace. Yet he saw this did not matter at all to God, who still poured out upon him his favors. Because Brother Lawrence accepted himself, God too accepted him. This was the meaning of forgiveness to Brother Lawrence. He would have understood Msimangu, young native priest of Alan Paton's African novel, *Cry, the Beloved Country:* "I am a weak and sinful man, but God put His hands on me, that is all." He took no pride in his sins; he certainly was not fascinated by them. Nor did he talk about them, mentioning them either in detail or in generality. He merely confessed his faults, then turned his back upon them.

He could do this, in the second place, because he knew God's love for him. In spite of his awkwardness and his common faults, he had received nothing but good from God all through his years in the monastery. So he was quick to accept God's love, finding in it strength more than sufficient to help him, either in practicing some virtue or in hindering him from further sin. No wonder he could then turn his back upon his sin and be ready to move along as though nothing had happened. And nothing *had* happened, as far as any kind of barrier being erected between himself and God. So Brother Lawrence peaceably resumed his usual practice of love and adoration.

Let us note for ourselves how this twofold acceptance of himself and of God's forgiveness speaks to us today.

For one thing, Brother Lawrence was not discouraged by his constant falling into difficulty. It was his nature ("I am used to do so"), and God understood him. So after he had confessed, he went on, not even pleading for forgiveness. He knew he was forgiven. After all, it was his custom to fail in his duty, especially when left to himself—and even with God's help too. So he had no qualms, for he knew God would be with him. From God and God alone did he find his strength.

For another thing, he expected to fall. He had a realistic

understanding of man. "That when we enter upon the spiritual life, we should consider and examine to the bottom what we are. And then we should find ourselves worthy of all contempt, and not deserving indeed the name of Christians; subject to all kinds of misery and numberless accidents, which trouble us and cause perpetual vicissitudes in our health, in our humors, in our internal and external dispositions; in short, persons whom God would humble by many pains and labors, within as well as without. After this we should not wonder that troubles, temptations, oppositions, and contradictions happen to us from men. We ought, on the contrary, to submit ourselves to them, and bear them as long as God pleases, as things highly beneficial to us." (4C, 15, p. 188.)

This was no unnecessary downgrading of himself and others. As he looked out upon his world, he saw just what the headlines in today's newspapers reveal: "That as for the miseries and sins he heard of daily in the world, he was so far from wondering at them that, on the contrary, he was surprised that there were not more, considering the malice sinners were capable of; that, for his part, he prayed for them; but knowing that God could remedy the mischiefs they did, when He pleased, he gave himself no further trouble" (1C, 9, p. 182).

How could he give himself "no further trouble"? Because man did not bear his burden alone. "We cannot escape the dangers which abound in this life," he wrote, "without the actual and *continual* help of God. Let us, then, pray to Him for it *continually.*" (10L, 4, p. 202.)

Remember how Christian, in *Pilgrim's Progress,* weighted down with his burden, looked up to a cross upon a hill, and his burden fell away? So the old gospel song spoke:

> At the cross, at the cross
>   where I first saw the light,
> And the burden of my heart rolled away,
> It was there by faith

> I received my sight,
> And now I am happy all the day!

This Brother Lawrence knew with certainty. "That we ought without anxiety to expect the pardon of our sins from the blood of Jesus Christ, laboring simply to love Him with all our hearts. That God seemed to have granted the greatest favors to the greatest sinners, as more signal monuments of His mercy." (2C, 18, p. 185.)

Here is the final conclusion of Brother Lawrence. Man is nothing; God is everything. "That the worst that could happen to him would be to lose that sense of God which he had enjoyed so long; but that the goodness of God assured him that He would not forsake him utterly, and that He would give him strength to bear whatever evil He permitted to happen to him; and therefore that he feared nothing, and had no occasion to consult with anybody about his soul." (3C, 8, p. 186.)

To Paul, to Augustine, to Brother Lawrence—yes, to you and to me—here is the Good News of God, the granting of the greatest favors to the greatest of sinners. For this is the striking testimony of Jesus himself: "I came not to call the righteous, but sinners" (Mark 2:17).

Experiments in Thought and Action

1. Who really are you?
2. Have you learned to accept yourself as you really are, without alibi?
3. Do you know personally God's forgiveness?
4. Are you a member of a small group where you can share lovingly your and their confessions, each helping the other? Will you try to gather together such a group?
5. Is there something you need to confess to a minister or a counselor? Will you go to such a person and humbly make your confession?

12

Abandonment
to God

If anyone wants to follow in my footsteps, he must give up all right to himself, take up his cross and follow me. (Mark 8:34 Phillips.)

So therefore, whoever of you does not renounce all that he has cannot be my disciple. (Luke 14:33.)

He who loves father or mother more than me is not worthy of me; and he who loves son or daughter more than me is not worthy of me; and he who does not take his cross and follow me is not worthy of me. He who finds his life will lose it, and he who loses his life for my sake will find it. (Matt. 10:37-39.)

I appeal to you therefore, brethren, by the mercies of God, to present your bodies as a living sacrifice, holy and acceptable to God, which is your spiritual worship. Do not be conformed to this world but be transformed by the renewal of your mind, that you may prove what is the will of God, what is good and acceptable and perfect. (Rom. 12:1-2.)

That perfect abandonment to God was the sure way to heaven, a way on which we had always sufficient light for our conduct. (3C, 8, p. 186.)

*I know that for the right practice of it the heart must be empty of all else, because God wills to possess the heart **alone**; and as He cannot possess it **alone** unless it be empty of all besides, so He cannot work in it what He would, unless it be left vacant to Him. (3L, 2, p. 194.)*

That we ought, once for all, heartily to put our whole trust in
God, and make a full surrender of ourselves to Him, secure that
He would not deceive us. (4C, 10, p. 188.)

One of the major teachings of Brother Lawrence is the
necessity of abandoning oneself to God. Because it is so important, to him and to us, in the opening of ourselves to the action
of God's grace, it will be dealt with at some length in Part
Three. Nevertheless, it belongs as one of the basic twelve practices through which God grants us a sense of his presence, so
that it must be considered briefly now.

Christian commitment is saying Yes to the light, the light
of God's love as revealed in Jesus. Man's highest happiness
is to face that light and to walk in it. This is to do God's will.

How can we do his will, though, when we do not know it?
Here is when Brother Lawrence speaks directly to us, for, said
he, it is "a way on which we had always sufficient light for our
conduct." He did not argue about God's will; he did not complain that he just could not understand it; he did not sigh that
it was too difficult. He said forthrightly: "We ought to give
ourselves up entirely to God, with regard both to things temporal and spiritual, and seek our satisfaction only in the fulfilling of His will, whether He leads us by suffering or consolation, for all would be equal to a soul truly resigned" (1C, 8, p.
182).

Of course we cannot *know* God's will in full. We are finite
creatures. Yet we can *do* it, for this is our task. We can take
the one step we do know, then the next, and each step will lead
to another. As we give up all right to ourselves, the steps will
be easier to take, the way easier to see. For we will not be
following our own way. We will be following his.

When I walk with a friend and pay attention to him, I realize
his presence. We talk together, or walk in silence, the inner
depths of our friendship speaking to each other. But when I

walk with him and do not pay attention, dreaming within myself or wandering far afield with my thoughts, I do not hear him speak—I do not notice his actions. I might just as well not be walking with him, for actually I am not, except in a physical sense. If he too is wrapped in the thin blanket of his own concern, not paying attention to me, we walk together, but in different worlds. There is no sense of presence, no sense of communion between us.

This is the way it is when I go along my way, thinking only of myself, thinking only of my desires, thinking only of my "rights." Though God is walking along with me, he never hides himself from me; I hide myself from him—there is no communion between us. I am alone, utterly alone, in the captivity of self. I possess me and am possessed by me. There can be no sense of presence.

Yet "God wills to possess the heart *alone*," Brother Lawrence said. His love is to be my love, his life is to be my life, his truth is to be my truth. What will happen to me I do not know. Whether suffering or consolation will follow, I do not know. I must trust him, trust that he does love me, that he knows what is best for me, that his love and his truth and his beauty and his justice are enough for me. Of all else I must be empty, so that he may possess me.

Can I trust that far? Dare I place myself without reservation in his hands, trusting in his goodness? This is the way of surrender, of abandonment, a way of trust that says willingly, "Here am I. Take me. Live in me. Like Paul, I would live; yet not I; but the Christ of God, let him live in me."

God will not deceive us. Brother Lawrence rested securely in this. From the time he first entered the monastery he had known nothing but the goodness of God. Suffering, sorrow, joy, peace—these and more he had known, but never once did he fail to trust God. "You must know that during the forty years and more that he has spent in religion, his continual care has been to be *always with God;* and to do nothing, say nothing, and think nothing which may displease Him, and this without any other view than purely for the love of Him, and because He deserves infinitely more" (2L, 2, p. 192).

How great this love of his; yet how God deserves every bit of it and more! Can we ever love him sufficiently? Can we ever give him the love we wish to give to him? No matter how much we do give, in the depths of our being, we know it is not enough. Yet it is. For God wants only what we have and what we are. Such is his love to us as he offers his presence to us. He does not wait until we are "worthy" of his love. As soon as we turn toward him, he is there. As soon as we begin to drag our weary steps homeward, he runs to meet us.

For eighty short years Brother Lawrence knew this love of God. Everything that God brought to him, he accepted in love, for the gifts were God's gifts to him. Hence, he could climax the last days of his life in an awareness of God's presence so strong that he did not care what happened to him; he knew it would only be good. The week before he died, he wrote to his favorite mother in Christ: "God knoweth best what is needful for us, and all that He does is for our good. If we knew how much He loves us, we should always be ready to receive equally and with indifference from His hand the sweet and the bitter" (16L, 1, p. 206).

So Brother Lawrence said Yes to the light, with an abandonment that rested trustingly in the love of God.

Experiments in Thought and Action

1. Can you trust God far enough to say to him Here I am. Take me. Live in me?
2. What are you holding back from God? Is there any portion of your life that you believe he does not want?
3. Are you willing to "give up all right" to yourself? What does this mean to you?

13
Meditations on Heaven, Hell, and Death

O Lord, our Lord,
how majestic is thy name in all the earth!

Thou whose glory above the heavens is chanted
by the mouth of babes and infants,
thou hast founded a bulwark because of thy foes,
to still the enemy and the avenger.

When I look at thy heavens, the work of thy fingers,
the moon and the stars which thou hast established;
what is man that thou art mindful of him,
and the son of man that thou dost care for him? (Ps. 8:1-4.)

And I heard a voice from heaven saying, "Write this: Blessed are the dead who die in the Lord henceforth." "Blessed indeed," says the Spirit, "that they may rest from their labors, for their deeds follow them!" (Rev. 14:13.)

For to me to live is Christ, and to die is gain. If it is to be life in the flesh, that means fruitful labor for me. Yet which I shall choose I cannot tell. I am hard pressed between the two. My desire is to depart and be with Christ, for that is far better. But to remain in the flesh is more necessary on your account. Convinced of this, I know that I shall remain and continue with you all, for your progress and joy in the faith, so that in me you may have ample cause to glory in Christ Jesus, because of my coming to you again. (Phil. 1:21-26.)

Then I saw a new heaven and a new earth; for the first heaven and the first earth had passed away, and the sea was no more. And I saw the holy city, new Jerusalem, coming down out of heaven from God, prepared as a bride adorned for her husband; and I heard a great voice from the throne saying, "Behold, the dwelling of God is with men. He will dwell with them, and they shall be his people, and God himself will be with them; he will wipe away every tear from their eyes, and death shall be no more, neither shall there be mourning nor crying nor pain any more, for the former things have passed away." (Rev. 21:1-4.)

For the first years I commonly employed myself during the time set apart for devotion with the thought of death, judgment, heaven, hell, and my sins. Thus I continued some years, applying my mind carefully the rest of the day, and even in the midst of my business, to the Presence of God, whom I considered always as with me, often as in me. (6L, 4, p. 197.)

That all bodily mortifications and other exercises are useless, except as they serve to arrive at the union with God by love. (2C, 16, p. 184.)

That the goodness of God assured him that He would not forsake him utterly, and that He would give him strength to bear whatever evil He permitted to happen to him; and therefore that he feared nothing, and had no occasion to consult with anybody about his soul. That when he had attempted to do it, he had always come away more perplexed; and that as he was conscious of his readiness to lay down his life for the love of God, he had no apprehension of danger. (3C, 8, pp. 186.)

For some time she sat very quietly. Then with wonder on her face she said: "Isn't life strange? We're here just a few days, and it's all over. Our friends are gone, our family is broken. And then there's nothing but pain. It's hard to find any meaning in it, isn't it?"

Her brother had died, a close friend had moved to a distant state, her son had lost his health, and now she was in the

first stages of a crippling disease. More than her own personal
life, though, was at stake, she well knew. With violence increasing between peoples and races and nations, with wars and
rumors of wars at hand, with involvement in almost anything
except "me and mine" coming to an end, she found it all a
strange wonderment. "Surely there is more than tragedy for
the whole world," she pondered.

What would you say? Have you found meaning for your
life, a purpose in it? Or do you find nothing in man except
a hopeless existence in this life?

One young woman in her late twenties, overwhelmed by the
blackness of her day, sought light in the physical return of
Jesus on a cloud. "If I did not have that hope with me every
moment of the day, I could not live," she declared. So she
waited day after day for God to intervene, a hope as ancient
as that of the Greek tragedians with their *deus ex machina*.

Brother Lawrence did not wait for God's intervention. He
found him close at hand in every experience. "I know not what
God purposes with me, or keeps me for; I am in a calm so
great that I fear nought. What can I fear, when I am with
Him? And with Him, in His Presence, I hold myself the
most I can. May all things praise Him. Amen." (7L, 3, p. 199.)

For ten years, though, no calm touched him, only trouble
and disquiet. In his first years in the monastery he followed the
practice of his colleagues in meditating upon death, judgment,
heaven, hell. The founders of his Order wanted no sentimental
brothers feeding on religious pap. Think on death and its certainty, the inevitability of judgment, the tortures of hell, the
glories of heaven—these will turn one from useless sentimental-
ity to a strong and realistic understanding of life. (How
different this is from our "feeding" of our young these days.
For her fourteen-year-old daughter a mother bought a copy
of *My Dear Ego* by Fritz Künkel, a stiff self-examination for
teen-agers. She read it herself first, though, then rejected it,

saying: "This is not for my daughter. I want something inspirational and easy!")

Of course, we are not taught to meditate on these themes today, for our culture is quite different. The principle, though, is valid. What is the meaning of my life? Where can I find purpose revealed in it? Is there more than tragedy to our brief day? Is there a heaven and a hell? Can I escape judgment? What is my highest happiness? These are not idle questions, nor are they for the idle. Only as one asks these and searches for answers, will he stand on the edge of meaning.

Nor is it enough to know the answers of others. Each one of us must find his own answers. Otherwise, they cannot be his.

Brother Lawrence puzzled over these for ten years, finding only trouble and disquiet. Perhaps the cause of his unrest, he thought, was his lack of devotion to God, or his many sins. "It seemed to me that all creation, reason, and God Himself were against me, and *faith* alone for me. I was troubled sometimes with thoughts that to believe I had received such favors was an effect of my presumption, which pretended to be *at once* where others arrive only with difficulty; at other times, that it was a wilful delusion, and that there was no salvation for me." (6L, 6, p. 197.)

What was wrong? Seemingly he continued his meditations beyond their usefulness. They were means to an end, to bring him into an awareness of God's presence. Yet all through the ten years he did have a sense of God's presence with him. Then suddenly one day he wrote, "I found myself changed all at once; and my soul, which till that time was in trouble, felt a profound inward peace, as if it had found its center of place of rest" (6L, 7, p. 197).

Did he no longer think of heaven and hell and death and judgment? Oh yes, but now in their rightful places, as means by which he could deepen and enlighten his continuing sense of presence. In themselves per se they were as nothing. Even physical mortifications, he said, were useless unless they helped bring about union with God.

When we begin to see this, we too will turn away from asking continually, What is the meaning of my life? We will not know it in full and probably never can know it in detail even for any one moment. Yet we will *know* that all is in God's hands and that the fulfillment of each day's tasks as duty calls us is our meaning—no troubled minds ill at ease in the world, defeated by the world. Rather, we will accept God's presence, live with that presence, and know his love. Questions still will be raised, and answers will continue to be rare; but they will not be as necessary as once we thought them. For we will have come to the final answer, that in God's love is our peace.

We will stop gossiping with others about the state of our religious life, wondering what is wrong with us, why we do not have an end to our doubts. Instead, we will know what and who we are with a realism equal to that of Brother Lawrence. Only we will also know with like certainty what and who God is. What else, then, can matter? For now we live by faith.

Then we too may say: "Ever since that time I walk before God in simple faith, with humility and with love, and I apply myself diligently to do nothing and think nothing which may displease Him. I hope that when I have done what I can, He will do with me what He pleases" (6L, 8, p. 198).

Experiments in Thought and Action

1. What is the meaning of your life?
2. Is there a common thread of purpose in it, upon which the beads of daily events, otherwise completely isolated, begin to show meaning?
3. What is your destiny?
4. Are you afraid of death? Why? Or why not?

14

Conversing
with God

Remember the wonderful works that he has done,
the wonders he wrought, the judgments he uttered,
O offspring of Abraham his servant,
sons of Jacob, his chosen ones! (I Chron. 16:12-13.)

Happy is the man who listens to me,
watching daily at my gates,
waiting beside my doors. (Prov. 8:34.)

I desire then that in every place the men should pray. (I Tim. 2:8.)

Rejoice in your hope, be patient in tribulation, be constant in prayer.
(Rom. 12:12.)

*He lays no great burden upon us: a little remembrance of Him
from time to time; a little adoration; sometimes to pray for His
grace, sometimes to offer Him your sorrows, and sometimes to
return Him thanks for the benefits He has given you, and still gives
you, in the midst of your troubles. He asks you to console yourself
with Him the oftenest you can. Lift up your heart to Him even
at your meals and when you are in company; the least little remembrance will always be acceptable to Him. You need not cry very
loud; He is nearer to us than we think. (5L, 1, p. 196.)*

*I do not advise you to use multiplicity of words in prayer; many
words and long discourses being often the occasions of wandering.*

*Hold yourself in prayer before God like a poor, dumb, paralytic beggar at a rich man's gate. Let it be **your business** to keep your mind in **the Presence of the Lord.** If it sometimes wanders and withdraws itself from Him, do not much disquiet yourself for that: trouble and disquiet serve rather to distract the mind than to recall it; the will must bring it back in tranquillity. If you persevere with your whole strength, God will have pity on you. (9L, 3, pp. 200-201.)*

That in this conversation with God we are also employed in praising, adoring, and loving Him unceasingly, for his infinite goodness and perfection. (4C, 3, p. 187.)

Here is the heart of the teaching of Brother Lawrence, the continual conversing with God, which is for him an actual presence of God. This we have already looked at in Part One. Because of its significance in growth in the life of prayer, further interpretation of this teaching will be presented in enlarged form in Part Three. Now, though, in this study of practices that open our minds and hearts to the grace of God, we will see that this is the one exercise above all others by which Brother Lawrence came into his sense of God's presence.

For him and for us it is exceedingly simple and equally easy. Yet it is a practice that few follow. Is it too simple, too obvious? Is it too naïve for this sophisticated age? Is it too intimate a speech for people so impersonal in most of their relationships? Is it too direct, with nothing between man and God except love?

Or do we confuse prayer with multisyllable words and pious phrases, set in lengthy discourses? This we hear so often from the pulpit in so-called pastoral prayer that we come to believe our personal prayers should be similar. Hence, for many prayer as conversation means little more than a wordy exercise in telling God what we want, with occasional thanks for past favors.

True enough, this conversation is not to be a vapid and sentimental chitchat between buddies; nor is it to be addressed

to "that man upstairs," even though he may be "a living doll!"
Neither is it to be the pseudoromanticism of popular ditties that
sing of "My God and I go in the field together," and the like.
Familiarity does breed contempt, for such familiarity, I have
found, is mostly "big talk and little do."

Brother Lawrence sets us straight. God lays no great burden
on us. Only a little remembrance of him from time to time, a
thank-you from the heart, a sigh of contrition, whisper of love,
an embarrassed cry for forgiveness, a blessing lovingly spread
over another.

Rarely is this a spoken word. Under pressure of an intense
emotional experience Jesus did cry out: "Abba, Father, all
things are possible to thee; remove this cup from me; yet not
what I will, but what thou wilt" (Mark 14:36); and Thomas
did confess: "My Lord and my God!" (John 20:28). More
often, though, it is a feeling, the heart at work, like a thought
whispered into the air, a thank-you without knowing to whom
it is said, a bless-you that is scarcely remembered.

In truth it cannot be called conversation in the normal usage
of the term, with a give and take of listening and responding,
though elements of that are there. Rather, it is like the quick
glance beween two people long and happily married, the sudden
smile, the assurance of love unspoken, the desire just to be
near each other, in the same room or the same house. Sometimes
—and this is not as foolish as it may seem—it is almost like the
one-sided telephone conversation of a teen-ager as heard by
another, a drawn-out yes-s-s, a quick hunh! or an acquiescent
m-m-m, followed by a long pause. Yet it is just as real, an
awareness of another, a listening that is "watching daily at my
gates, waiting beside my door."

It is of the heart, not of the mind, of the feeling, not of the
intellect. It is a knowing that cannot be shaken.

Yet it begins with a simple prayer consciously uttered, the
flash prayer of our modern day, the ejaculatory prayer—the
spear thrust—of the ancients. Hurled into the air a hundred or

a thousand times a day, a *thank-you* makes a thankful heart; *I'm sorry* makes a contrite soul; a *bless-you* makes a loving spirit.

So a wandering pilgrim, seeking the prayer that is without ceasing, followed the advice of his starets, as told in *The Way of a Pilgrim*.[1] Repeating the simple Jesus Prayer of Greek Orthodox mysticism, "Lord Jesus Christ, have mercy on me," over and over again, he came to that oneness with God which Brother Lawrence had found two hundred years before. He prayed consciously until unknowingly he became the prayer. It was a secret, continual conversing between two who loved. Through this kind of prayer Brother Lawrence too became the prayer and in it found the presence of God.

Experiments in Thought and Action

1. Write a conversational prayer, as though you are talking directly to your Father.
2. Now write the other side of the conversation, what the Father is saying to you.
3. Act upon it.

---

[1] Trans. from the Russian by Reginald M. French (New York: Seabury Press, 1962).

15

Dependence
upon God

Trust in the Lord with all your heart,
   and do not rely on your own insight. (Prov. 3:5.)

Thou dost keep him in perfect peace,
   whose mind is stayed on thee,
   because he trusts in thee. (Isa. 26:3.)

Truly, truly, I say to you, the Son can do nothing of his own accord, but only what he sees the Father doing; for whatever he does, that the Son does likewise. . . . I can do nothing on my own authority; as I hear, I judge; and my judgment is just, because I seek not my own will but the will of him who sent me. (John 5:19, 30.)

I can do all things in him who strengthens me. (Phil. 4:13.)

But he said to me, "my grace is sufficient for you, for my power is made perfect in weakness." I will all the more gladly boast of my weaknesses, that the power of Christ may rest upon me. For the sake of Christ, then, I am content with weaknesses, insults, hardships, persecutions, and calamities; for when I am weak, then I am strong. (II Cor. 12:9-10.)

That when an occasion of practising some virtue offered, he addressed himself to God, saying, Lord, I cannot do this unless thou enablest me; and that then he received strength more than sufficient. (2C, 5, p. 183.)

*That God always gave us light in our doubts when we had no
other design but to please him, and to act for His love. (4C, 5,
p. 187.)*

*That the greater perfection a soul aspires after, the more dependent
it is upon divine grace. (4C, 16, p. 188.)*

God is sovereign, not man. God is the creator, man the
created. God is at the center of life, man at the periphery.

Even though in his knowledge and skill man far surpasses
all other animals so that his exploits are the continuing surprise
of the wisest of all, still he cannot stand on his own. His dependence is upon God. In God does he find the source of truth
and justice and love and beauty, not in himself. When the
springs of God flood man's spirit, he knows he is but a vessel,
that from God himself justice rolls "down like waters, and
righteousness like an everflowing stream" (Amos 5:24).

To channel this stream into the empty lives of others Brother
Lawrence first recognized his own emptiness. How could he
reveal to others the love, the joy, the patience of God, when
he was so unloving, so joyless, so impatient? So when the
opportunity came, within the monastery itself, or in the world at
large, to practice some virtue, Brother Lawrence knew his own
weakness. "Lord, I cannot do this unless Thou enablest me,"
he said. Then the power came, for he received strength more
than sufficient to meet whatever need awaited him.

Like Paul before him Brother Lawrence knew the perverse-
ness of man. Within himself he just did not have the will power
to do what he knew he should do. What he wanted to do, he
could not do without outside help. Hence, "When he had
failed in his duty, he simply confessed his fault, saying to God,
*I shall never do otherwise if Thou leavest me to myself; it is
Thou who must hinder my falling, and mend what is amiss.*
That after this he gave himself no further uneasiness about it"
(2C, 6, p. 183).

Then why should he be bothered? He was no longer working alone. God was with him. In no way, though, does this presuppose that Brother Lawrence had turned everything over to a benevolent God, who would then take full charge. He still carried on his work day by day, doing what he knew he must do; but he had help, God's strength, an inflowing of the spirit that always means a sufficiency. Not that it could be measured, of course; Brother Lawrence found that because of this inflowing strength, he now could succeed in his duties.

He did not believe foolishly that God would do his work for him. He learned to wait, finding in his inner conversation with God a sense of power that came from the certainty of God's presence. Then, in the light of that presence, he moved ahead, knowing always that his inability to perform his duties was matched by God's help. Consider how Brother Lawrence set forth upon his wine-buying expeditions. It was business that he did not like—business for which he had no special talent. Nevertheless, "he gave himself no uneasiness about it, nor about the purchase of the wine. That he said to God, *It was His business he was about,* and that afterwards he found it very well performed" (2C, 8, p. 183). It was God's business, so Brother Lawrence did the best he could—and God saw that it was well done.

The catch, of course, is knowing whether or not our business is God's business. If we are certain it is God's business, then we can do it as best we can, knowing that he will accept our effort. But suppose it is not God's business? Will our failure reveal this? Or might we through native talent bring it to a successful conclusion?

We just cannot know for certain, for to know his will for certain is to be God. We are finite; he is infinite. Yet Brother Lawrence believed he could know God's will in accepting direction from a superior, in fulfilling the duties that were laid before him. This we too can know.

"I'm just not the kind of mother I ought to be," she said.

Instead of turning away from her motherly duties, though, she persevered in them, believing God had called her to them as a mother. Consequently, though she was never satisfied that she was always doing the very best she could do, at the moment she did the best she could then do and found it acceptable. She decided to leave the outcome to him, believing that he would take the best she could give. Though she had never heard of Graham Taylor, she made her religion to be what the noted Chicago clergyman defined as "making the most of ourselves and doing the best by others."

Always such a search for a more perfect way of fulfilling one's duties reveals to oneself his own inadequacies. Just how can I achieve the high goal that life holds before me? In myself I have only what life has placed there, and it seems so little. Yet God's grace, always reaching out to me, offers that "more than extra," that all-sufficiency. What Paul had learned in Corinth, Brother Lawrence learned in Paris. No wonder he could say with simple trust: "That the greater perfection a soul aspires after, the more dependent it is upon Divine Grace."

Experiments in Thought and Action

1. Who is at the center of your life? Just what do you mean by your answer? Be as honest as you can.
2. From your own experience describe how you have been able to "do all things in him who strengthens" you.

16

No Vain Regrets
for His Sin

Bear fruits that befit repentance, and do not begin to say to yourselves, "We have Abraham as our father"; for I tell you, God is able from these stones to raise up children to Abraham. Even now the ax is laid to the root of the trees; every tree therefore that does not bear good fruit is cut down and thrown into the fire.

And the multitudes asked him, "What then shall we do?" And he answered them, "He who has two coats, let him share with him who has none; and he who has food, let him do likewise." Tax collectors also came to be baptized, and said to him, "Teacher, what shall we do?" And he said to them, "Collect no more than is appointed you." Soldiers also asked him, "And we, what shall we do?" And he said to them, "Rob no one by violence or by false accusation, and be content with your wages." (Luke 3:10-14.)

For even if I made you sorry with my letter, I do not regret it (though I did regret it), for I see that that letter grieved you, though only for a while. As it is, I rejoice, not because you were grieved, but because you were grieved into repenting; for you felt a godly grief, so that you suffered no loss through us. For godly grief produces a repentance that leads to salvation and brings no regret, but worldly grief produces death. (II Cor. 7:8-10.)

Remember then from what you have fallen, repent and do the works you did at first. If not, I will come to you and remove your lampstand from its place, unless you repent. (Rev. 2:5.)

99

*That when an occasion of practising some virtue offered, he ad-
dressed himself to God, saying,* **Lord, I cannot do this unless
thou enablest me;** *and that then he received strength more than
sufficient. (2C, 5, p. 183.)*

*That when he had failed in his duty, he simply confessed his
fault, saying to God,* **I shall never do otherwise if Thou leavest
me to myself; it is Thou who must hinder my falling, and
mend what is amiss.** *That after this he gave himself no further
uneasiness about it. (2C, 6, p. 183.)*

*That when sometimes he had not thought of God for a good while,
he did not disquiet himself for it; but after having acknowledged
his wretchedness to God, he returned to Him with so much the
greater trust in Him as he had found himself wretched through
forgetting Him. (3C, 1, p. 185.)*

*When he had finished he examined himself how he had discharged
his duty; if he found* **well,** *he returned thanks to God; if otherwise, he asked pardon; and without being discouraged, he set his
mind right again, and continued his exercise of the* **Presence of
God,** *as if he never had deviated from it. "Thus," said he, "by
rising after my falls, and by frequently renewed acts of faith and
love, I am come to a state wherein it would be as difficult for me
not to think of God as it was at first to accustom myself to it."
(4C, 23, p. 189.)*

*Yet I must tell you that for the first ten years I suffered much.
The apprehension that I was not devoted to God as I wished to be,
my past sins always present to my mind, and the great unmerited
favors which God bestowed on me, were the matter and source of
my sufferings. During this time I fell often, yet as often rose again.
It seemed to me that all creation, reason, and God Himself were
against me, and* **faith** *alone for me. I was troubled sometimes
with thoughts that to believe I had received such favors was an
effect of my presumption, which pretended to be* **at once** *where
others arrive only with difficulty; at other times, that it was a
wilful delusion, and that there was no salvation for me.*

When I thought of nothing but to end my days in these times of trouble and disquiet (which did not at all diminish the trust I had in God, and which served only to increase my faith), I found myself changed all at once; and my soul, which till that time was in trouble, felt a profound inward peace, as if it had found its center and place of rest.

Ever since that time I walk before God in simple faith, with humility and with love, and I apply myself diligently to do nothing and think nothing which may displease Him. I hope that when I have done what I can, He will do with me what He pleases. (6L, 6-8, pp. 197-98.)

In Chapter 11 we examined "Confession of Sin" as one of the practices of Brother Lawrence. We learned how he came to accept both himself and God's forgiveness, so that he could place "his sins betwixt him and God." In this we saw our own need to confess our faults, to accept ourselves as we really are, to accept God's forgiveness for us.

To confess one's sins, though, then to hold on to them with increasing guilt, is to lead oneself into a psychotic state. Brother Lawrence came very close to falling into this trap. For ten long years he suffered much, able readily to confess his sins and to admit the truth about himself, but he was unable to let go of them. Finally, when he had decided that trouble and disquiet were to be his the rest of his days, he found himself suddenly changed. No longer did vain regret for his sins fasten themselves upon him.

How often we are like the young mother, attending a quiet day in her church, who forgot to pick up her daughter at the close of kindergarten. When suddenly she remembered the child, she hurried to find her, apologizing for being a half-hour late. "Mama's little darling, I'm so sorry, please forgive me," she asked. The two returned to the church, picked up a younger child left in the day-care center, and started for home. Again

the mother, upset by her forgetfulness, apologized to the kinder-
gartner. Her daughter looked at her and said, "Mother, I
forgave you. Why don't you forget it?" She was forgiven—
why hold on to it?

Of course, if our problem were as simple as our shame in
forgetting a child for a moment, we would have no problem.
It is remembering day in and day out the sin we committed,
the word we spoke in anger, the letter we should never have
mailed, the prejudice we seemingly cannot control. If only
we had not done this evil thing!

Or as happens often with those who have accepted a
discipline within a prayer class or for their personal devotions
or for their outreach of service—they become so busy and
usually with necessary and good things (is it ever otherwise?)
that they forget their well-intentioned discipline. To beat oneself then with regret and condemnation is futile. Brother
Lawrence at times seemed to forget God; yet he did not become
discouraged. He just confessed once again his wretchedness,
then dropped it.

Yet it took him ten years to overcome this futile regret and
self-condemnation. He kept asking himself the same questions
we ask today: "Am I really devoted to God as much as I wish
to be? If I were truly Christian, would I do things like that?
Surely I am better than this." In part at least, both for Brother
Lawrence and for ourselves, we are caught by our self-conceit:
"I, being who I am, with the commitment that is mine, ought
not to act like that. I must be chief of sinners."

Then this state of pride is compounded by the realization
that through it all, God still pours out his favors upon us, gifts
wholly unmerited by us. With Angelus Silesius of three centuries ago we ask:

> How cometh it to pass
> that into such as me

Floweth Almighty God,
into one drop the sea? [1]

Brother Lawrence wondered if he had truly received such favors. Was it just his presumption that made him think he had? Was his inner peace only a numbness of spirit? Was his sense of the presence of God only a figment of his imagination? Either he was a supreme egotist, pretending "to be *at once* where others arrive only with difficulty"; or it was all "a wilful delusion; and that there was no salvation" for him. Perhaps into the sea of himself had come only a drop of Almighty God.

How, then, did he overcome this vain regret? He stopped fighting it. The more one fights against a regret, bringing it to mind over and over again, the more it fastens itself to the mind. He said that he probably would end his days in such trouble and disquiet, and he accepted the fact. Then he went a step further. He continued his trust in God. His acceptance of the situation "did not at all diminish the trust I had in God," he wrote. Rather, it "served only to increase my faith." In other words, he had committed himself in full surrender intellectually; now he actually surrendered himself into God's hands, regrets or no regrets. Then he found release. "My soul, which till that time was in trouble, felt a profound inward peace, as if it had found its center and place of rest."

Does that mean for us today that we must wait ten years? Hardly, though it is possible. It means we must learn to trust ourselves, even the tendency to hang on to our regrets, to his love. We will rise and we will fall. But in our rising and in our falling God is there, faithful, holy, loving.

No longer worrying about ourselves, no longer in the depths of despair one day, on the heights of ecstasy another, we will come to a new experience of self-understanding, in which, like Brother Lawrence, we may say: "I walk before God in simple

---

[1] Johann Scheffler (Angelus Silesius, pseud.), *The Cherubinic Wanderer* (New York: Pantheon Books, 1953), p. 30.

faith, with humility and with love, and I apply myself diligently to do nothing and think nothing which may displease Him. I hope that when I have done what I can, He will do with me what He pleases."

Experiments in Thought and Action

1. What regrets still linger in your mind as you recall a sin? Have you sought the forgiveness of persons involved? Have you sought God's forgiveness?
2. Why do you still hold to these? Is it your conceit, that you, being who you are, ought really *not* to behave like that?
3. Are you willing to give all of yourself, including all your regrets, to God's love? Will you do it by conscious act, even though there is seemingly no response from him?

17

Persistent Meditation
Until the Need Is Ended

And when he knocked at the door of the gateway, a maid named Rhoda came to answer. Recognizing Peter's voice, in her joy she did not open the gate but ran in and told that Peter was standing at the gate. They said to her, "You are mad." But she insisted that it was so. They said, "It is his angel!" But Peter continued knocking; and when they opened, they saw him and were amazed. (Acts 12:13-16.)

Not that I have already obtained this or am already perfect; but I press on to make it my own, because Christ Jesus has made me his own. Brethren, I do not consider that I have made it my own; but one thing I do, forgetting what lies behind and straining forward to what lies ahead, I press on toward the goal for the prize of the upward call of God in Christ Jesus. (Phil. 3:12-14.)

Then two men will be in the field; one is taken and one is left. Two women will be grinding at the mill; one is taken and one is left. Watch therefore, for you do not know on what day your Lord is coming. But know this, that if the householder had known in what part of the night the thief was coming, he would have watched and would not have let his house be broken into. Therefore you also must be ready; for the Son of man is coming at an hour you do not expect. (Matt. 24:40-44.)

That at the beginning he had often passed his time appointed for prayer in rejecting wandering thoughts and falling back into them. That he could never regulate his devotion by certain methods

105

*as some do. That, nevertheless, at first he had **meditated** for some time, but afterwards that went off in a manner he could give no account of. (2C, 15, p. 184.)*

*It is, however, necessary to put our whole trust in God, laying aside all other cares, and even some particular forms of devotion, though very good in themselves, yet such as one often engages in unreasonably, because these devotions are only means to attain to the end. So when by this **practice of the Presence of God** we are **with Him** who is **our End,** it is then useless to return to the means. (4L, 5, p. 195.)*

I know that to arrive at this state the beginning is very difficult, for we must act purely in faith. But though it is difficult, we know also that we can do all things with the grace of God, which He never refuses to them who ask it earnestly. Knock, keep on knocking, and I answer for it that He will open to you in His due time, and grant you all at once what He has deferred many years. (15L, 2, p. 206.)

I have quitted all forms of devotion and set prayers but those to which my state obliges me. And I make it my only business to persevere in His holy presence, wherein I keep myself by a simple attention, and an absorbing passionate regard to God. (6L, 10, p. 198.)

A member of a prayer class was puzzled. "Is something the matter with my praying? I used to spend an hour every day in meditation, but that time grows less each day. I just don't seem to need so much time. What am I doing wrong?"

She had accepted the discipline of the seventh practice of Brother Lawrence—daily meditation upon basic themes of her Christian faith. Through this she had come to understand meanings in her life that had been hidden to her earlier. Hence, she found the practice of daily meditation most helpful.

Only now she was disturbed, for she was not "completing" the full hour of former days. Gradually the time of meditation had grown less and less, until finally she noticed what was happening. "It seems that God is with me, and I just don't continue the meditation. I forget what I was thinking about. What should I do?" she asked.

"Tell God he came too soon," her minister said with a smile. "Tell him he isn't due for another few minutes!"

She grinned. "That's just what I was doing, wasn't it?" she said. "I was trying to finish the hour. I forgot that meditation was only a means to an end."

This was similar to the experience of Brother Lawrence. At first he practiced regular meditation too, finding it difficult to avoid distractions and wanderings; but in time this became easy for him. Then he found that such meditation disappeared in a manner that he could not account for.

This disturbed him, for he knew the value of this practice. Twenty years later, though, he could say: "These devotions are only means to attain to the end. So when by this *Practice of the Presence of God* we are *with Him* who is *our End,* it is then useless to return to the means."

This I have learned also. Using a biblical passage or a reading from one of the spiritual classics as the basis of my meditation, I found that suddenly I no longer was aware either of the reading or of my thinking upon it. Instead, I found I was resting in his love, in quiet and stillness. Sometimes there was a marked sense of his presence, but much of the time there was no praise or adoration, only a forgetfulness of self and time and place. No dreaming was in it, no ecstasy, no pleasure, or joy—only an assurance of companionship.

Like Brother Lawrence I have "quitted all forms of devotion and set prayers" except a stated time each day for reading a chapter from the New Testament, and from a portion of a classic, and for intercession for those regularly on my prayer list. Other than that, I find my whole day is caught up in little breathings of prayer, an "O Father" or a "Blessed be thy name," no special concern, and certainly nothing "wanted." It is like the quick "hello" to a friend, filled with intimacy and longing, but without that familiarity. Rather, it is the awesome awareness of presence in a friend, in an experience, in a remembrance —and sometimes, with no known cause, only a response to someone unseen but felt.

Experiments in Thought and Action

1. Does God always "speak" to you in your daily personal devotions? Do you sometimes "sow" the seed of meditation without a sense of its taking root? Are you then willing to "lie fallow" until the seed does sprout?
2. Is the length of your meditation period becoming shorter and shorter? Is this because of your refusal to take time? Or because of an increasing awareness throughout the day of his presence?

18

Do All Work
for the Love of God

So, whether you eat or drink, or whatever you do, do all to the glory of God. (I Cor. 10:31.)

Whatever you do, in word or deed, do everything in the name of the Lord Jesus, giving thanks to God the Father through him. . . . Whatever your task, work heartily, as serving the Lord, and not men. (Col. 3:17, 23.)

As each has received a gift, employ it for one another, as good stewards of God's varied grace: whoever speaks, as one who utters oracles of God; whoever renders service, as one who renders it by the strength which God supplies; in order that in everything God may be glorified through Jesus Christ. (I Peter 4:10-11.)

"Master, I knew you to be a hard man, reaping where you did not sow, and gathering where you did not winnow; so I was afraid, and I went and hid your talent in the ground. Here you have what is yours." But his master answered him, "You wicked and slothful servant! You knew that I reap where I have not sowed, and gather where I have not winnowed? Then you ought to have invested my money with the bankers, and at my coming I should have received what was my own with interest. . . . Cast the worthless servant into the outer darkness; there men will weep and gnash their teeth." (Matt. 25:24-27, 30.)

Having accustomed himself to do everything there for the love of God, and with prayer, upon all occasions, for His grace to do his

109

work well, he had found everything easy during the fifteen years that he had been employed there. (2C, 9, p. 184.)

That with one single end in view, he did all for the love of God, rendering Him thanks for that He had directed these acts, and an infinity of others throughout his life. (3C, 5, p. 186.)

*That the most excellent method he had found of going to God was that of **doing our common business** without any view of pleasing men, and (as far as we are capable) **purely for the love of God.** (4C, 7, p. 187.)*

That we ought not to be weary of doing little things for the love of God, who regards not the greatness of the work, but the love with which it is performed. (4C, 11, p. 188.)

*We can do **little** things for God. I turn the cake that is frying on the pan for love of Him, and that done, if there is nothing else to call me, I prostrate myself in worship before Him, who has given me grace to work; afterwards I rise happier than a king. It is enough for me to pick up but a straw from the ground for the love of God. (4C, 21, p. 189.)*

It was observed that in the greatest hurry of business in the kitchen, he still preserved his recollection and heavenly-mindedness. He was never hasty nor loitering, but did each thing in its season, with an even, uninterrupted composure and tranquillity of spirit. "The time of business," said he, "does not with me differ from the time of prayer, and in the noise and clatter of my kitchen, while several persons are at the same time calling for different things, I possess God in as great tranquillity as if I were upon my knees at the Blessed Sacrament." (4C, 24, p. 190.)

An American churchwoman, visiting mission stations in Africa, asked a native to describe his Christian work. "I'm a baker," he said.

"No," she said, "I mean what do you do in the church?"

Again he replied, "I'm a baker."

"I'm sorry. You misunderstand me," she continued. "I want to know what you do as a Christian."

"You misunderstand me!" he answered. "I am a baker. That is how I am a Christian." [1]

She expected him to tell the offices he held, the tasks within the church that he handled. This for her was his Christian work, something done "within" the church. He knew better. His Christian work was his day-by-day work, the work of a baker.

Here is the strength of Brother Lawrence. He was not a professional "religious," given orders by the church. He was a lay brother, one who accepted voluntarily, without orders, the rule and life of a monastery. Always free to leave if he wished, he chose to give his life to God in the manual labor of his community. Hence, anything and everything he did, working in the fields and the stables, serving as cook and kitchen helper, buying wine for the house, everything was a task lovingly done for his God. Not as a monk or an inmate of a monastery, not as a church school teacher or choir singer or board member, did he serve. All his labor, his "common business," was done for the love of God.

It was very well done, too. An old proverb has it that "if it is worth doing at all, it is worth doing well." Often my mother used it as an incentive to her children to do well whatever their tasks might be, small or large. Malvina Hoffman, America's finest woman sculptor, learned this from a childhood friend, Dr. Bennett Nash, then professor of classical languages at Harvard, who spent his summers where the Hoffman family vacationed in Maine. He helped her with various carvings, including a jewel box made for her mother.

---

[1] This may be an apocryphal tale, for Dr. George MacLeod tells a similar story about a Scots baker and a Scots clergyman. Nevertheless, a real truth is revealed here.

Professor Nash took infinite pains to show me just how to miter the corners, countersink the hinges, and sandpaper every edge, even though these were to be covered by the leather lining. "Remember, Mallie, that the Japanese craftsmen stand out above others because of the perfection of their workmanship. They even carve the underside of bases and boxes, where only a few eyes ever discover their hidden, delicate designs. We Americans forget that the angels can see through and around and under just as well as from the front." [2]

Equally true, though, is this statement: "If it is worth doing, it is worth doing badly." No preacher worth his salt has ever believed at the close of a sermon that he has finally "made it." He wishes he truly could have done well! But under the circumstances, he has done as well as he could, believing that God wanted his workmanship, even if it was not very fine. What he had to offer, that he offered in love.

This is not an excuse for slovenly work. Though not very well done, according to some technical standards, the work will be the best that at the moment the individual can do. He will not try to "get by."

In another passage Miss Hoffman tells of one whose work was much like that of Brother Lawrence, menial labor in cleaning and preparing the studios of various sculptors. Yet Bill had unusual ability as an artist too, she discovered. This he flatly denied. He stated firmly,

"No, not good *enough*. It didn't take me long to know my work was second class, maybe third, maybe steerage, and it made me sick. I wanted tops or nothing, so I decided to work in some artists' studios to help them out, posing and kneading their clay and cleaning floors, studying all the time to see what the heck art was all about. When I fix up the clay into nice fat little sausages, just the right consistency, I says to meself—If ye can't do it yerself,

[2] From *Yesterday Is Tomorrow* by Malvina Hoffman, p. 40. © 1965 by Malvina Hoffman. Used by permission of Crown Publishers.

at least you can grease the wheels for the other guy and help him to climb to dizzy heights!"

When I suggested that he ought to break in a young assistant to carry on "the Bill technique," he shouted at me, "Hell, Lady, none of the kids today know what work means and they don't plan to find out, either. I tell you it's sweat and elbow grease and love o' beauty in me own special way that got me where I am. The kids today try to get by, leavin' out all they can, so maybe the boss won't see behind things or around the corner. But I start off with the bad corners and back o' things, so I know when the furniture is pushed back it's setting on clean ground. That gives me a kick. To hell whether the boss sees it. A good boss will notice just that sort of performance, and if he doesn't, well, I'll damn well drag him over one day and make him look behind things, and he'll say, 'Bill, it's beautiful,' and on my way home I'll feel so lighthearted I'll blow the first poor guy I meet to a beer!" [3]

Brother Lawrence did his work for the love of God, whereas Bill did his for the love of beauty. Were they not brothers of the spirit?

Experiments in Thought and Action

1. How much of your work is drudgery to you?
2. Would you rather your son were to be a garage mechanic or a doctor of medicine? Do you think either choice would be "preferable" to God? Why? Or why not?
3. What arguments can you offer that the work of a clergyman or missionary is more significant that that of a businessman or a housewife? Are these arguments valid?

[3] *Ibid.*, p. 172.

PART THREE

A CALL
TO A MATURING FAITH

Introduction

It must be very evident now that the utter simplicity of Brother Lawrence is completely unlike that of the sentimental and unrealistic person who says so piously: "All we need to do is to pray, and everything will be well." Such a person just does not understand the world in which he lives. His prayer is almost magic, phrases said to appease an angry God or to cajole an uncertain one. Such praying is foolishness in today's world.

Brother Lawrence won his simplicity after years of trial, for his first ten years in the monastery were particularly a time of much suffering. Yet he continued faithfully the twelve practices described in Part Two, until he suddenly found himself changed all at once, as though his soul had gained a "center and place of rest." We can achieve a like simplicity too, but only after facing the difficulties and trials that this contemporary world forces upon us. The experiments in thought and action that conclude each of the twelve chapters of Part Two are to help us do that very thing.

Now we go a step further. Behind these twelve practices are basic ideas which point to a maturing faith. They are as valid today as they were in the time of Brother Lawrence. Unless we can understand them and accept them and live by them, we shall be caught in an immature faith that makes prayer a game to be played, Christianity a cloak to be put on.

We are not called to a blind faith, a "Try again. Draw a long breath and shut your eyes" of the Queen in *Alice in Wonderland*. Nor is it a sentimental faith based on a "nice" feeling. Brother Lawrence did not love God because he had been "good" to him. He knew nothing of a "quid pro quo" relationship.

His was a maturing faith, experiential, obedient, robust. He offered no pap to spiritual babes. He offered strong meat to the growing spirit. Without the learning of a Meister Eckhart of an earlier century or of a Jean de Caussade of a later one, Brother Lawrence in his simplicity of speech and action yet revealed himself as much a nobleman of God as the former, as much *l'abandonné* as the latter.[1]

It is to such a maturing faith that Brother Lawrence through his writings calls us today.

[1] Cf. "The Aristocrat" in *Meister Eckhart* and de Caussade's *Self-Abandonment to Divine Providence*.

19

A High Notion
of God

In the beginning God. (Gen. 1:1.)

Behold, the Lord our God has shown us his glory and his greatness. (Deut. 5:24.)

> Great is the Lord, and greatly to be praised,
> and his greatness is unsearchable. (Ps. 145:3.)

> I form light and create darkness,
> I make weal and create woe,
> I am the Lord, who do all these things. (Isa. 45:7.)

For it is the God who said, "Let light shine out of darkness," who has shone in our hearts to give the light of the knowledge of the glory of God in the face of Christ. (II Cor. 4:6.)

Then I heard what seemed to be the voice of a great multitude, like the sound of many waters and like the sound of mighty thunderpeals, crying,

> "Hallelujah! For the Lord our God
> the Almighty reigns." (Rev. 19:6.)

He received a high view of the providence and power of God, which has never since been effaced from his soul. (1C, 2, p. 181.)

That we should feed and nourish our souls with high notions of

God, which would yield us great joy in being devoted to Him.
(1C, 6, p. 181.)

*He told me that the **foundation of the spiritual life in him**
had been a high notion and esteem of God in faith: which when he
had once well conceived, he had no other care but faithfully to
reject at once every other thought, **that he might perform all his
actions for the love of God.** (3C, 1, p. 185.)*

*That in the beginning of his novitiate he spent the hours appointed
for private prayer in thinking of God, so as to convince his mind
of, and to impress deeply upon his heart, the divine existence, rather
by devout sentiments, and submission to the lights of faith, than
by studied reasonings and elaborate meditations. That by this short
and sure method he exercised himself in the knowledge and love of
God, resolving to use his utmost endeavor to live in a continual
sense of His Presence, and, if possible, never to forget Him more.*

*That when he had thus in prayer filled his mind with great senti-
ments of that Infinite Being, he went to his work appointed in
the kitchen. (4C, 18-19, p. 189.)*

*At other times, when I apply myself to prayer, I feel all my spirit
and all my soul lift itself up without any trouble or effort of mine,
and it remains as it were in elevation, fixed firm in God as in its
center and its resting-place. (6L, 13, p. 198.)*

A God small enough to manipulate is not worth having.
When his services are available to the highest "pray-er," a
handy man hired by the performance of certain religious duties,
he is no more than the creature of man's desire. Like the gods
of varying powers of more primitive peoples, he is to be accepted when he answers my prayer, rejected when he fails to
answer it.

What I mean by "answer," of course, is that I get what I
want. If I do not get it, then he does not answer me. The basis
of such judgment rests solely upon my getting what I want.

Hence, God is only a tool of my desire, to bring me a "yes" answer. I cannot recognize what I call an "unanswered" prayer as a "no" answer.

Brother Lawrence, so far ahead of most of our generation, would be horrified by such thinking. To him God was no superficial minor deity, to be cajoled into giving a petitioner whatever he wanted. While still a youth, Brother Lawrence "received a high view of the providence and power of God," never to be effaced throughout his long life. Constantly he fed his soul upon this high notion of God. He, Brother Lawrence, was the creature; God was the creator. Brother Lawrence did not try to usurp the place of God. Only God was God.

Not a hint of a suggestion is there, in the Conversations or Letters, that Brother Lawrence ever once tried to manipulate God. Rather, God is the End in himself, not the means to whatever end we may choose. Brother Lawrence, "since his first coming to the monastery . . . had considered God as the *end* of all his thoughts and desires, as the mark to which they should tend, and in which they should terminate" (4C, 17, p. 189). So all he asked for was a continuing sense of God's presence. He had everything else he needed. Hence, when he was beyond seventy-five years of age and probably no longer able to work in the kitchen, he wrote "I know not what God purposes with me, or keeps me for; I am in a calm so great that I fear nought. What can I fear, when I am with Him?" (7L, 3, p. 199.) Later, in his eightieth year, he recalled the times when he thought he was dying. "I did not pray for any relief, but I prayed for strength to suffer with courage, humility, and love." (15L, 1, p. 206.)

And how could he do this? It was simple. He lived in paradise! "It is paradise to suffer and be with Him; so that if even now in this life we would enjoy the peace of paradise, we must accustom ourselves to a familiar, humble, affectionate conversation with Him." (15L, 1, p. 206.)

Some might say that is the sentimental thinking of a worn-

out old man readying himself for death. He was no longer
facing the tension of life.

How foolish! In his early days as a novitiate, when his
strength was equal to any task, he impressed deeply upon his
heart the greatness of God, "rather by devout sentiments, and
submission to the lights of faith, then by studied reasonings
and elaborate meditations." Out of this prayer he "filled his
mind with great sentiments of that Infinite Being," then went
to work as a cook. No petty God would have satisfied him. No
small God would have sustained him through the noise and
clutter of the kitchen. No God able to be manipulated would
have been great enough for this strong spirit.

How long has it been since you asked God anything for yourself? It has been many years since I have dared ask for myself,
and probably your experience has been like mine. How could
I ask when far more than I needed was at hand? Everything is
here just for the taking, God's gift to me, to all of us. So
Brother Lawrence did not try to use God as a means to
any kind of end for himself.

How about the needs of others, though? Did he not ask
God to do things for them? Here too Brother Lawrence shows
his maturing faith. He prayed for others, as many of his letters
reveal. Sometimes it was to give help to those trying to find a
sense of presence. "I will assist you with my prayers, poor as
they are." Sometimes it was to commend himself to the prayers
of others, and offer his own in return. Never, though, was it
to beg God's favor for something material.

To two nuns suffering from bodily ailments he offered advice. To one he wrote: "I do not pray that you may be delivered
from your troubles, but I pray God earnestly that He would
give you strength and patience to bear them as long as He
pleases. . . . Continue, then, always with God; it is the only
support and comfort for your affliction. I shall beseech Him to
be with you" (12L, 1, 7, pp. 203-4).

To the second nun he wrote much the same: "Take courage;

offer Him your pains unceasingly; pray to Him for strength to endure them. Above all, acquire a habit of conversing often with God, and forget Him the least you can. Adore Him in your infirmities, offer yourself to Him from time to time, and in the very height of your sufferings beseech Him humbly and affectionately (as a child his good father) to grant you the aid of His grace and to make you conformable to His holy will. I shall endeavor to help you with my poor halting prayers" (13L, 2, p. 204).

In a second letter to her a short time later, after expressing his sorrow for her grief, he goes a step further: "I told you in my last that He sometimes permits the body to suffer to cure the sickness of the soul. Have courage, then; make a virtue of necessity. Ask of God, not deliverance from the body's pains, but strength to bear resolutely, for the love of Him, all that He should please, and as long as He shall desire" (14L, 2, p. 205). He knew how difficult it was to pray like that: "a little hard to nature, but most acceptable to God." Yet he did not fail to call her beyond herself to a more mature faith.

In a time when bodily ailments seem to be at the center of a generation's life, such as is true with ours, it is wise to consider the words of Brother Lawrence. Not only with prayers for ourselves, but also with prayers for others, do we need to move beyond requests for specific help of a material kind. These may be "a little hard to nature," but certainly they will be "acceptable to God" as evidence of our maturing faith. For he is no little God to be used for our ends. He is that Infinite Being to whom we come in humility.

20

A God Worthy of
Our Self-Abandonment

The eternal God is your dwelling place,
   and underneath are the everlasting arms. (Deut. 33:27.)

O come, let us worship and bow down,
   Let us kneel before the Lord, our Maker! (Ps. 95:6.)

For as the heavens are higher than the earth,
   so are my ways higher than your ways,
   and my thoughts than your thoughts. (Isa. 55:9.)

Your Father knows what you need before you ask him. (Matt. 6:8.)

To the King of ages, immortal, invisible, the only God, be honor and glory for ever and ever. (I Tim. 1:17.)

To him who sits upon the throne and to the lamb be blessing and honor and glory and might for ever and ever! (Rev. 5:13.)

He answers with exact fidelity to these inward drawings, either by an elevation of his heart toward God, or by a meek and loving regard to Him; or by such words as love forms upon these occasions, as for instance, My God, behold me, wholly Thine: Lord, make me according to Thy heart. And then it seems to him (as in effect he feels it) that this God of love, satisfied with such few words, reposes again, and rests in the depth and center

of his soul. The experience of these things gives him such an as-
surance that God is always deep within his soul, that no doubt of
it can arise, whatever may betide. (2L, 4, p. 193.)

God knowest best what is needful for us, and all that he does is for
our good. If we knew how much He loves us, we should always be
ready to receive equally and with indifference from His hand the
sweet and the bitter. (16L, 1, p. 206.)

That we ought, once for all, heartily to put our whole trust in God,
and make a full surrender of ourselves to Him, secure that He
would not deceive us. (4C, 10, p. 188.)

Only to a God like the God of Brother Lawrence, high and
lifted up, would we give ourselves in self-abandonment. He
alone is worthy of that gift. It cannot be given to another. It
cannot be given to one less worthy.

At the same time, how can we dare to give ourselves in
abandonment to him? Because we can put our trust heartily in
him, knowing that he will not deceive us. He can be trusted with
every corner of our lives, those full of the light of his love and
those full of the darkness of our self-centeredness. For he, the
sovereign God, is a God of faithfulness, a God of love.

So Brother Lawrence believed, and so he trusted. Hence, it
was simple for him to offer himself in full surrender to such a
God.

For many people such a surrender smacks of fear, of the
power of a wrathful God forcing us to our knees against our
will. Not so with Brother Lawrence, who knew God as a God
of love, the light of whose countenance was his peace. With
complete confidence in the faithfulness of his God, Brother
Lawrence wrote: "That perfect abandonment to God was the
sure way to heaven, a way on which we had always sufficient
light for our conduct" (3C, 8, p. 186). God's love gave him
that light.

Too many of us hold a very low view of God. We are afraid of him, or think he is too far off or that he is really not interested in us or that he is quite impersonal or too small to handle our problems. Brother Lawrence had only a high notion of God, a loving one known intimately within, offering a constant sense of presence, willing to listen to anything, a faithful one from whom "we may beg His assistance for knowing His will in things doubtful, and for rightly performing those which we plainly see He requires of us" (4C, 2, p. 187).

This is fine, of course, when all is going well. What happens, though, when suffering comes, when problems seem insurmountable? Brother Lawrence was a realist, who based his trust on past experience in part. God was a great God, and, as such, he could not and would not deceive his children. When Brother Lawrence was fifty-five years old, he said, "That he expected hereafter some great pain of body or mind; that the worst that could happen to him would be to lose that sense of God which he had enjoyed so long; but that the goodness of God assured him that He would not forsake him utterly, and that He would give him strength to bear whatever evil He permitted to happen to him; and therefore that he feared nothing, and had no occasion to consult with anybody about his soul" (3C, 8, p. 186).

For Brother Lawrence believed in the providence of God. There was no magic in it, no superstition that somehow God would protect him from all harm. This he knew was false. Rather, if God loved him, as Brother Lawrence knew he did, then truly "underneath are the everlasting arms." How, then, could he be disturbed by whatever happened? After all, God was the sovereign God—all power, all might, all purpose, all love in his hands. Yet he, Brother Lawrence, was God's man.

True enough, he was only a cook, an ordinary lay brother in a small monastery. Yet at the same time he was God's man, to whom M. Beaufort came that he, a Grand Vicar, might learn better to serve God; to whom others wrote, that they might learn of God's great gift to him of the constancy of his presence. It was God, a great God, that Infinite Being, who gave meaning to Brother Lawrence's life, making him God's man.

Three hundred years later Dietrich Bonhoeffer, a man of vast learning, a theologian whose teachings influence so many today, knew something of the same experience. In those last few weeks of prison before his execution by the Nazis, Bonhoeffer wrote:

WHO AM I?

Who am I? They often tell me
I stepped from my cell's confinement
calmly, cheerfully, firmly,
like a Squire from his country house.

Who am I? They often tell me
I used to speak to my warders
freely and friendly and clearly,
as though it were mine to command.

Who am I? They also tell me
I bore the days of misfortune
equably, smilingly, proudly,
like one accustomed to win.

Am I then really that which other men tell of?
Or am I only what I myself know of myself?
Restless and longing and sick, like a bird in a cage,
struggling for breath, as though hands were compressing
my throat,
yearning for colours, for flowers, for the voices of birds,
thirsting for words of kindness, for neighbourliness,
tossing in expectation of great events,
powerlessly trembling for friends at an infinite distance,
weary and empty at praying, at thinking, at making,
faint, and ready to say farewell to it all.

Who am I? This or the Other?
Am I one person to-day and to-morrow another?
Am I both at once? A hypocrite before others,
and before myself a contemptible woebegone weakling?
Or is something within me still like a beaten army
fleeing in disorder from victory already achieved?

Who am I? They mock me, these lonely questions of mine.
Whoever I am, Thou knowest, O God, I am thine! [1]

With similar insight into the worthiness of the God whom
he loved, Brother Lawrence, a week before his death at age
eighty, expressed his own trust in one who would not deceive
him. "If we knew how much He loves us, we should always
be ready to receive equally and with indifference from His
hand the sweet and the bitter." (16L, 1, p. 206.)

[1] From *The Cost of Discipleship* (paper ed.; New York: The Macmillan
Company, 1963), pp. 18-20. Used by permission of The SCM Press.

21

A Full Surrender
of Ourselves

For thou hast no delight in sacrifice;
  were I to give a burnt offering,
    thou wouldst not be pleased.
The sacrifice acceptable to God is a broken spirit:
  a broken and contrite heart, O God, thou wilt not despise.
  (Ps. 51:16-17.)

And I heard the voice of the Lord saying, "Whom shall I send, and who will go for us?" Then I said, "Here I am! Send me." (Isa. 6:8.)

And to love him with all the heart, and with all the understanding, and with all the strength, and to love one's neighbor as oneself, is much more than all whole burnt offerings and sacrifices. (Mark 12:33.)

Remove this cup from me; yet not what I will, but what thou wilt. (Mark 14:36.)

If, after all these years, I were still courting the favour of men, I should not be what I am, the slave of Christ. (Gal. 1:10 Knox.)

As obedient children, do not be conformed to the passions of your former ignorance, but as he who called you is holy, be holy yourselves in all your conduct; since it is written, "You shall be holy, for I am holy." (I Peter 1:14-16.)

That perfect abandonment to God was the sure way to heaven, a way on which we had always sufficient light for our conduct. (3C, 8, p. 186.)

*I know that for the right practice of it the heart must be empty of all else, because God wills to possess the heart **alone;** and as He cannot possess it **alone** unless it be empty of all besides, so He cannot work in it what He would, unless it be left vacant to Him. (3L, 2, p. 194.)*

I know that to arrive at this state the beginning is very difficult, for we must act purely in faith. But though it is difficult, we know also that we can do all things with the grace of God, which He never refuses to them who ask it earnestly. (15L, 2, p. 206.)

That we ought, once for all, heartily to put our whole trust in God, and make a full surrender of ourselves to Him, secure that He would not deceive us. (4C, 10, p. 188.)

Once again I return to the pregnant phrase that we ought to "make a full surrender of ourselves to Him." We can trust this God, for he will not deceive us, as we have found in the preceding chapter. Earlier, though, in Part Two, Chapter 12, we saw that this same phrase was the key to the practice of self-abandonment by Brother Lawrence, in which he discovered a continuing sense of God's presence.

This is because of his great love for God. Brother Lawrence did not feel forced into this surrender, as already I have pointed out. It was the free gift of an appreciative, thankful heart to a loving God. He was glad to be like Paul, a slave of Christ.

For Brother Lawrence this offering of himself was an act of love. True love is always an offering. True love, Christian love, does not try to get. Plato says love is to get, and much of our loving is a getting. Unless we get something in return for our love, most of us will stop loving. Christian love, though, is a giving, not a getting. This is true love, an offering of the self, the whole self, in full surrender to the one loved.

True prayer is also an offering of the self. Beginning prayer, immature prayer, is often a seeking for something, a "give me" or a "help me." True prayer, though, is the complete and total offering of the self to the God to whom we pray.

Hence, true prayer, maturing prayer, an offering of the self, is "Here I am! Send me." True love, maturing love, an offering of the self, is "Not what I will, but what thou wilt." In Brother Lawrence this true prayer and this true love are combined in his single phrase—"a full surrender of ourselves to Him."

Both are an offering, an offering of love. Nothing can be withheld. "You cannot serve God and mammon." So Brother Lawrence writes: "I know that for the right practice of it the heart must be empty of all else, because God wills to possess the heart *alone;* and as He cannot possess it *alone* unless it be empty of all besides, so He cannot work in it what He would, unless it be left vacant to Him" (3L, 2, p. 194).

This emptying of the heart, with its sign "Reserved for God alone," is not the selflessness of a blur or a blob, in which one becomes a nonentity, forever losing his own personality, his his own individuality. These are gifts from God. It is as Nels F. S. Ferré has said, a "self-fullness," the whole self given over to God's use and direction, that total, unique personality that is ours lived to the full, as far as our understanding of God permits.

It is Abram, going out without knowing where he is going, but confident that God would direct his entire action. It is Moses, leaving the security of a pastoral idyl to demand that Pharaoh let God's people go. It is David, penitently offering his last years as a psalm sung to the Lord. It is Francis of Assisi, accepting marriage to Lady Poverty with a joy unknown to a world caught in material goods.

In more recent years it is Eugene V. Debs, sick in heart if one other is sick, imprisoned in heart if one other is in prison. It is Norman Thomas, leaving a comfortable pulpit to attack politically poverty, tyranny, and provincialism. It is Harry Emerson Fosdick, resigning a pulpit rather than compromising with truth. It is Albert Schweitzer, conscience-stricken by man's inhumanity to the African, building a tin-roof hospital in the Congo.

None of these men, then or now, knew completely the will of God for himself, nor did a single one of them turn away from the unique personality God had given him. Each used what he had, but no longer for himself. He gave what he had in service to One greater than himself. Each was changed at the center of his being, as Florence Allshorn wrote: "Just as lying in the sun doing nothing, surrendering your body to it, with the sun blazing down on you, affects your body and your senses, so this surrendering of the soul to that transforming Power affects the soul, and I believe that as truly as the sun changes the colour of your skin so that Power changes you at the centre." [1]

Brother Lawrence was a child of his own day. He felt no call to another country, no inner demand to fight politically and economically and religiously for human justice, no deep desire to stand for peace in a warring world, to speak the truth in a time of bigotry. He withdrew into a monastery as a lay brother. Yet he is one with these others, men who gave themselves in full surrender to the One who alone possessed their hearts. Each went his way as that way was marked out for him by his heritage, his environment, his capacities, his talent, his opportunities. Each in his own manner, according to his understanding of the God whom he served, did as Brother Lawrence did: "I engaged in a religious life only for the love of God, and I have endeavored to act only for Him; *whatever becomes of me, whether I be lost or saved,* I will always continue to act purely for the love of God. I shall have this good at least, that till death I shall have done all that is in me to love Him" (2C, 2, p. 183, italics mine).

---

[1] J. H. Oldham, *Florence Allshorn* (New York: Harper & Brothers, 1952), p. 141.

22

Do Not Seek God
for His Favors

"We are setting out for the place of which the Lord said, 'I will give it to you'; come with us, and we will do you good; for the Lord has promised good to Israel." But he said to him, "I will not go; I will depart to my own land and to my kindred." And he said, "Do not leave us, I pray you, for you know how we are to encamp in the wilderness, and you will serve as eyes for us." (Num. 10:29-31.)

"The Son of man came not to be served but to serve, and to give his life as a ransom for many." (Matt. 20:28.)

I can do nothing on my own authority; as I hear, I judge; and my judgment is just, because I seek not my own will but the will of him who sent me. (John 5:30.)

Slaves, be obedient to those who are your earthly masters, with fear and trembling, in singleness of heart, as to Christ; not in the way of eye-service, as men-pleasers, but as servants of Christ, doing the will of God from the heart, rendering service with a good will as to the Lord and not to men. (Eph. 6:5-7.)

That he was pleased when he could take up a straw from the ground for the love of God, seeking Him only, and nothing else, not even His gifts. (2C, 1, p. 182.)

I engaged in a religious life only for the love of God, and I have endeavored to act only for him; whatever becomes of me, whether

I be lost or saved, I will always continue to act purely for the love of God. (2C, 2, p. 183.)

But that with one single end in view, he did all for the love of God, rendering Him thanks for that He had directed these acts, and an infinity of others throughout his life. (3C, 5, p. 186.)

It is not pleasure which we ought to seek in this exercise; but let us do it from the motive of love, and because God would have us so walk. (3L, 3, p. 194.)

Let us not content ourselves with loving God for the mere sensible favors, how elevated soever, which He has done or may do us. Such favors, though never so great, cannot bring us so near to Him as faith does in one simple act. (16L, 3, p. 207.)

A man asked: "Why should I pray? I don't want anything." How would you answer him? Is not the chief object of prayer to get something? That is what God is for, to give us what we want. Hence, we will not bother him, will not seek him, when we have no needs.

Huysman, knowing human nature, evidently believed the same way when he wrote: "The rich, the healthy, the happy seldom pray." Why should they? They have everything they want; they have no physical ailments; they are on top of the world! Why should they seek God?

Folk who think like that are caught in a twofold immaturity. First, they believe that God is very little more than an oversize Santa Claus, a celestial bellhop waiting for their call. And second, they believe that prayer is only asking God for something.

With concern for both of these, Brother Lawrence calls us to a faith beyond the point that most of us are willing to go. Already we have examined his high notion of God, seeing something of his understanding of the providence and power of the Infinite Being whom he knew deep within himself with an almost constant sense of presence. This sovereign God, high and lifted up, he knew with an intimacy as rare then as it is today.

At the same time Brother Lawrence discovered that prayer is far, far more than asking God for something. That prayer in part is petition, he would be the first to affirm. Yet this "converse with God," in which "we may beg His assistance for knowing His will in things doubtful, and for rightly performing those which we plainly see He requires of us," is, with Brother Lawrence, supplemented by "offering them to Him before we do them, and giving Him thanks when we have done." Even more, though, is involved, for he added, "That in this conversation with God we are also employed in praising, adoring, and loving Him unceasingly, for His infinite goodness and perfection" (4C, 2, 3, p. 187).

With his understanding of the greatness of God, it was inevitable that Brother Lawrence should move far beyond petition to obedience to God's will through trust and love, an obedience undergirded by praise and adoration. He just could not possibly think of attempting to use God for any means whatever, even seemingly good and devout ones. "It is not pleasure which we ought to seek in this exercise," he wrote. No, it is to be practiced "from the motive of love, and because God would have us so walk." No ulterior motive, no matter how saintly, would satisfy him. God is an End in himself, never a means to a smaller end. That is why everything Brother Lawrence did was for the love of God—and for that alone.

Yet how we do serve God for his gifts. Or pray to him for gain. Let the gifts become fewer in number, let the gain begin to decrease, and we are ready to switch gods, or worse yet, to give him up as worthless. "I prayed, and didn't get an answer," we say. "That's enough for me!"

Such a phrase is no worse, though, than those that seem pious like: "Pray, and you'll always be well"; or "Tithe faithfully, and you'll be prosperous"; or "When you move, attend church in your new community, and you'll always find friends";

or "Read the Bible, and you'll never get into trouble." To
Brother Lawrence these near-blasphemous phrases would be as
silly as the popular sentence: "A family that prays together
stays together." He would have laughed, though with a heart-
sickness in his laughter, at a judge who foolishly sentences a
probationer to church attendance every Sunday for six months.

God is to be sought for himself, not for any sensible gifts
whatever—just to pick up a straw from the ground because it
is there and needs picking up. Not to win God's favor or to earn
his gifts. Just out of love for him, "seeking Him only, nothing
else, not even His gifts."

Nor even for himself. So Meister Eckhart wrote that there
should be no "reason" whatever for serving God:

Do all you do, acting from the core of your soul, without a single
"why." I tell you, whenever what you do is done for the sake of
the Kingdom of God, or for God's sake, or for eternal blessing,
and thus really for ulterior motives, you are wrong. You may pass
for a good person, but this is not the best. For, truly, if you
imagine that you are going to get more out of God by means of
religious offices and devotions, in sweet retreats and solitary orisons,
than you might by the fireplace or in the stable, then you might
just as well think you could seize God and wrap a mantle around
his head and stick him under the table! To seek God by rituals
is to get the ritual and lose God in the process, for he hides behind
it. On the other hand, to seek God without artifice, is to take him
as he is, and so doing, a person "lives by the Son," and is the
life itself.[1]

That is how God would have us walk. How difficult, though,
for us, who love God because of what he does for us (or may
do) ; who want a church in our community, whether we attend
or not, because real estate values are then higher; who fear
God's wrath, so that we attend church regularly to escape from

[1] Raymond Bernard Blakney, trans., *Meister Eckhart* (Torchbooks ed.;
New York: Harper & Brothers, 1941), p. 127.

hell, with no thought of loving him; who seek an emotional experience rather than a sustaining faith; who want above all a peace of mind that will make everything fall into place.

No wonder Meister Eckhart, student of human nature that he was, further wrote:

Some people want to see God with their eyes as they see a cow and to love him as they love their cow—they love their cow for the milk and cheese and profit it makes them. That is how it is with people who love God for the sake of outward wealth or inward comfort. They do not rightly love God when they love him for their own advantage. Indeed, I tell you the truth, any object you have on your mind, however good, will be a barrier between you and the inmost truth.[2]

What the preacher and scholar and theologian of the thirteenth century wrote in picturesque phrase, the simple lay brother of the seventeenth century knew with equal insight: "It is not pleasure which we ought to seek in this exercise; but let us do it from the motive of love, and because God would have us so walk."

What a stretch of mind and heart Brother Lawrence demands of us today.

[2] *Ibid.*, p. 241.

23

An Oratory
of the Heart

For thus says the high and lofty One
   who inhabits eternity, whose name is Holy:
"I dwell in the high and holy place,
   and also with him who is of a contrite and humble spirit,
to revive the spirit of the humble,
   and to revive the heart of the contrite." (Isa. 57:15.)

I do not pray for these only, but also for those who are to believe in me through their word, that they may all be one; even as thou, Father, art in me, and I in thee, that they also may be in us. (John 17:20-21.)

For we are the temple of the living God; as God said,
        "I will live in them and move among them,
        and I will be their God,
        and they shall be my people." (II Cor. 6:16.)

No man has ever seen God; if we love one another, God abides in us and his love is perfected in us. (I John 4:12.)

To be with God, there is no need to be continually in church. We may make an oratory of our heart wherein to retire from time to time to converse with Him in meekness, humility, and love. Every one is capable of such familiar conversation with God, some more, some less. He knows what we can do. Let us begin, then. (5L, 2, p. 196.)

I say again, let us enter into ourselves. Time presses, there is no room for delay; our souls are at stake. You, I believe, have taken such effectual measures that you will not be surprised. I commend you for it; it is the one thing needful. We must, nevertheless, always work at it, for, in the spiritual life, not to advance is to go back. But those whose spirits are stirred by the breath of the Holy Spirit go forward even in sleep. If the vessel of our soul is still tossed with winds and storms, let us awake the Lord, who reposes in it, and He will quickly calm the sea. (2L, 8, p. 193.)

Let us seek Him often by faith. He is within us; seek Him not elsewhere. (16L, 3, p. 207.)

Brother Lawrence spoke of "the providence and power of God," an Infinite Being far beyond the comprehension of finite man. Yet more than almost any other teacher of Christian piety, he taught and exemplified in his own life the indwelling of God's presence. Though he did not use the word "immanence," he lived with the experience as a daily certainty. At the very close of his life he wrote with confidence to an old friend: "Let us seek Him often by faith. He is within us; seek Him not elsewhere."

How frantically some people search for God. They go from church to church, looking for a minister who is "spiritual." They attend retreat after retreat, conference after conference, meetings of the Camps Farthest Out, the Ashrams, the Disciplined Order of Christ, hoping to find in the words of some leader the answers to their searching. They read book after book, believing that in some devotional text suddenly the way will be opened to them. Sometime, somewhere, in a manner that may be strikingly dramatic, from outside of themselves will come a revelation of God.

Yet God always makes himself known within us. Evidences of the creative spirit whom we call God, the Infinite Being of Brother Lawrence, may be seen in the wonder and mystery of nature, in the events of history, in the experiences of human nature, especially in human love and justice. Intimations of his reality are to be found in the world of the arts—music, literature, painting, sculpture, architecture, even the dance. Still, it is within us that we know him, and only within us.

Early Brother Lawrence learned this, and within his innermost being he made his little oratory, to which he retired as his work permitted, there conversing humbly and lovingly with his God. He went to church, as we have already noted; that is, he regularly attended the stated services of his monastery. Yet it was unnecessary for him to wait until arriving there to find God. He took with him to these services his inner sense of presence, his awareness of God. But whether in church or not, whether at work or at leisure, Brother Lawrence never was away from his God. For his God was as close as the oratory of his heart.

It was his continual conversation with God, "praising, adoring, and loving Him unceasingly," an abiding fellowship with his God through prayer, that made this sense of presence possible. He knew within himself what Meister Eckhart had written so long before: "Thou needst not call Him to thee from a distance; thy opening and His entering are but one moment: it is harder for Him to wait, than for thee." When my daughter was very small, I escorted her across a busy street. As we came to the curbing, I reached down to take her hand just as she reached up to take mine. That is what Eckhart is meaning—"thy opening and His entering are but one moment"!

Everyone, Brother Lawrence wrote, is capable of such a familiar conversation. "Let us enter into ourselves." From that well of experience will come an inner quiet, a tranquillity, a leisureliness that will be a puzzlement to others.

Almost three hundred years later Walter Rauschenbusch, renowned teacher of social ethics, discovered within himself "a little postern gate" through which he could enter his own "oratory of the heart."

THE LITTLE GATE TO GOD

In the castle of my soul
Is a little postern gate,
Whereat, when I enter,
I am in the presence of God.
In a moment, in the turning of a thought,
I am where God is,
This is a fact.

. . . .

When I enter into God,
All life has a meaning,
Without asking I know;
My desires are even now fulfilled,
My fever is gone
In the great quiet of God.
My troubles are but pebbles on the road,
My joys are like the everlasting hills.

. . . .

So it is when my soul steps through the postern gate
Into the presence of God.
Big things become small, and small things become great.
The near become far, and the future is near.
The lowly and despised is shot through with
 glory. . . .
God is the substance of all revolutions;
When I am in Him, I am in the Kingdom of God.
And in the Fatherland of my Soul.[1]

[1] From the *Pilgrim Hymnal*. Copyright, 1931, 1935, The Pilgrim Press. Used by permission.

24

A Little Lifting Up
of the Heart

Seek the Lord and his strength,
  seek his presence continually! (I Chron. 16:11.)

Every day I call upon thee, O Lord;
  I spread out my hands to thee. (Ps. 88:9.)

And he told them a parable, to the effect that they ought always to pray and not lose heart. (Luke 18:1.)

Pray at all times in the Spirit, with all prayer and supplication. (Eph. 6:18.)

Let him think of Him as often as he can, especially in the greatest dangers. A little lifting up of the heart suffices. A little remembrance of God, one act of inward worship, though upon a march and sword in hand, are prayers which, however short, are nevertheless very acceptable to God; and far from lessening a soldier's courage in occasions of danger, they best serve to fortify it. (8L, 2, p. 200.)

That in order to form a habit of conversing with God continually, and referring all we do to Him, we must at first apply to Him with some diligence; but that after a little care we should find His love inwardly excite us to it without any difficulty. (2C, 3, p. 183.)

That we should not wonder if, in the beginning, we often failed in our endeavors, but that at last we should gain a habit, which will naturally produce its acts in us, without our care, and to our exceeding great delight. (4C, 11, p. 188.)

*In short, by often repeating these acts, they become **habitual**, and the **Presence of God** is rendered as it were **natural to us**. (1L, 4, p. 192.)*

We must, nevertheless, always work at it, for, in the spiritual life, not to advance is to go back. (2L, 8, p. 193.)

A woman, concerned for a wounded soldier, sought advice from Brother Lawrence. Recognizing that the soldier was a courageous and brave lad, of good disposition and good will, yet still "of the world and a great deal of youth," Brother Lawrence hoped the affliction might be used as a time for reflection, especially of taking stock. Whether the lad became morose or gay would depend wholly upon his own choice.

Perhaps out of his own soldiering experience Brother Lawrence gave him simple counsel. "Let him think of Him as often as he can, especially in the great dangers. A little lifting up of the heart suffices. A little remembrance of God, one act of inward worship, though upon a march and sword in hand, are prayers which, however short, are nevertheless very acceptable to God; and far from lessening a soldier's courage in occasion of danger, they best serve to fortify it."

Some people believe Brother Lawrence was not concerned with the practical. This statement should end that belief. Earlier, while working in the kitchen, while journeying on wine-buying trips, and even before that while toiling in the fields and stable, he was as mundane as could be. Though he did not reveal the "social concern" that is so prevalent in modern thought—the phrase had not even been thought of at that time—he had a real concern for God's presence in every affair of one's daily life. Hence, writing about a soldier who was recuperating before returning to service, Brother Lawrence suggested that he lift up quick, short prayers that not only would be most acceptable to God, but would also fortify him in times of danger.

The key sentence in his letter is "A little lifting up of the heart suffices." If we can learn the significance of this brief sentence, we will come a long ways toward acquiring the same sense of God's presence that Brother Lawrence had.

These short prayers are the ejaculatory prayers which have undergirded Christian devotion from the beginning. "Ejaculate" means to throw out or hurl—thus, a quick throwing out of prayer to God, darts of love so tiny, yet so meaningful. Today these are frequently called flash prayers, a little lifting up of the heart as quick and as bright as the flashbulb of the modern camera. They take no time at all, require no special place, no particular posture. In the midst of one's business or his leisure, in times of fatigue or early-morning briskness, in moments called "nonreligious" as well as "religious," these prayers are little remembrances of God, simple acts of inward worship. No one else will know of them, for the eyes remain open and the lips are still.

They are quick thanksgivings, simple *God-bless-you's,* sudden *please-forgive-me's,* quiet breathings of adoration, seldom spoken aloud, yet offered ten times a day, a hundred times, deepening the awareness of God's presence, acknowledging that presence with whispers of prayer. For myself I can testify that with the practice of these prayers through the years, at first deliberately and consciously done, then later a very part of me, I have come to feel wonder and awe before the Eternal, touched with warmth and affection as between friends.

Thomas Kelly, sensitive Quaker of a past generation, learned that time and place had nothing to do with this lifting up of the heart.

I must confess that it doesn't take time, or complicate your program. I find that a life of little whispered words of adoration, of praise, of prayer, of worship can be breathed all through the day. One can have a very busy day, outwardly speaking, and yet be steadily in the holy Presence. . . .

There is a way of life so hid with Christ in God that in the midst of the day's business one is inwardly lifting brief prayers, short ejaculations of praise, subdued whispers of adoration and of tender love to the Beyond that is within. . . . One can live in a well-nigh continuous state of unworded prayer, directed toward God, directed toward people and enterprises we have on our heart. There is no hurry about it all; it is a life unspeakable and full of glory, an inner world of splendor within which we, unworthy, may live.[1]

A YMCA secretary, overly busy with a line of boys waiting at his desk, unable to "center down" because of the multiplicity of problems they brought to him, lost his sense of the inner presence. Then he excused himself from the waiting line and walked to the water cooler. While getting his drink, he lifted the boys in prayer before God, a simple trust in his love. With renewed insight, having turned from his own inadequacy to God's adequacy, he went back to his boys. Only a moment passed, but in that moment he touched reality within, finding strength and refreshment.

A warning, though. This is no game to play; it is a life to live. It may begin by directed efforts, deliberate attempts to practice this inward worship. It must go on, though, until it is as unconscious as breathing. We must work at it, until it becomes habitual. "That in order to form a habit of conversing with God continually, and referring all we do to Him, we must at first apply to Him with some diligence; but that after a little care we should find His love inwardly excite us to it without any difficulty."

That great teacher of prayer, Francis de Sales, Bishop of Geneva, who lived not too far from Brother Lawrence and

[1] *A Testament of Devotion* (New York: Harper & Brothers, 1941), pp. 120, 122.

whose days overlapped, understood well the importance of such inward conversation.

Now, as the great work of devotion consists in the exercise of spiritual recollection and ejaculatory prayers, the want of all other prayers may be supplied by them; but the loss of these can scarcely be repaired by any other means. Without them we cannot lead a good, active life, much less a contemplative one. Without them repose would be but idleness and labor vexation. Wherefore, I conjure you to embrace this, exercise your whole heart, without ever desisting from its practice.

Such prayer is the prayer that is without ceasing. Practiced continually, day in and day out, it becomes our very life, not a word spoken, not a word thought, but a word lived.

25

Know God
to Love Him!

Can you find out the deep things of God?
Can you find out the limit of the Almighty? (Job 11:7.)

Let us know, let us press on to know the Lord. (Hosea 6:3.)

They shall not hurt or destroy
in all my holy mountain;
for the earth shall be full of the knowledge of the Lord
as the waters cover the sea. (Isa. 11:9.)

Holy Father, keep them in thy name which thou hast given me, that they may be one, even as we are one. (John 17:11.)

Simon, son of John, do you love me? (John 21:16.)

If any one imagines that he knows something, he does not yet know as he ought to know. But if one loves God, one is known by him. (I Cor. 8:2-3.)

For now we see in a mirror dimly, but then face to face. Now I know in part; then I shall understand fully, even as I have been fully understood. (I Cor. 13:12.)

We cannot escape the dangers which abound in life without the actual and **continual** *help of God. Let us, then, pray to Him for it* **continually.** *How can we pray to Him without being with Him? How can we be with Him but in thinking of Him often? And how can we often think of Him unless by a holy habit of thought* *which we should form? You will tell me that I am always saying the same thing. It is true, for this is the best and easiest method I know; and as I use no other, I advise all the world to do it. We must **know** before we can **love**. In order to **know** God, we must often **think** of Him; and when we come to **love** Him, we shall then also think of Him often, for our heart will be with our treasure. This is an argument which well deserves your consideration. (10L, 4, p. 202.)*

*Let all our business be to **know** God; the more one **knows** Him, the more one **desires** to know Him. And as **knowledge** is commonly the measure of **love**, the deeper and more extensive our **knowledge** shall be, the greater will be our **love**; and if our love of God be great, we shall love Him equally in grief and in joy. (16L, 2, pp. 205-6.)*

Who can *know* God? Our finite minds find it impossible to comprehend him; yet at the same time they can apprehend him. Baron Friedrich van Hugel has said it succinctly: "God, our own souls, all the supreme realities and truths, supremely deserving and claiming our assent and practice, are both incomprehensible and indefinitely apprehensible, and the constant vivid realization of these two qualities is of primary and equal importance for us."

In a different way Paul wrote something of the same thought in his letter to the Corinthians: "If anyone imagines that he knows something, he does not yet know as he ought to know. But if one loves God, one is known by him."

Brother Lawrence believed that to love God we must know him. Was he simpleminded? I think not. He was writing out of the experience of a lifetime. "We must know before we can love," he said. We begin with what we know, small though that be, and it will then grow, for "knowledge is commonly the measure of love."

How can this be? By "a holy habit of thought," that constant practice of the presence through conversing with him, the "little lifting up of the heart" of our last chapter. Of course, Brother Lawrence is repeating himself; this he admitted: "You will tell me that I am always saying the same thing. It is true, for this is the best and easiest method I know; and as I use no other, I advise all the world to do it."

Recall, also, the high notion that Brother Lawrence had of the providence and power of God. Not to him would J. B. Phillips address his book, *Your God Is Too Small*. To Brother Lawrence God came first, above all others, before all others. He rejected any thought that might in any way limit his high esteem for God. So in his very last letter he returns to this, from which he never could go very far: "Let all our business be to *know* God; the more one *knows* Him, the more one *desires* to know Him."

Long before Brother Lawrence's time, Anselm, one of the great teachers and thinkers of the church, wrote: "Truly indeed I see not that light, which is too bright for me; and yet whatever I see, I see by means of it, even as what the weak eye sees, it sees by means of the sun, though into the sun itself it may not look."

The simple monastery cook saw too by "that light," for it was "the true light that enlightens every man," including Brother Lawrence himself. Hence, he had grown beyond the need for argument, for questionings about God. We need to face this today. Who and what is God? Does he truly love us, truly care for us? Was John correct in saying that "God is love"? So we ask.

Brother Lawrence had gone beyond all this in his maturing faith. To know what he knew, little though that might be, was enough for him to love God. So it was he began his novitiate with no one having to teach him. Rather, as he told M. Beaufort, in those early days "he spent the hours appointed for private prayer in thinking of God, so as to convince his mind and to impress deeply upon his heart, the Divine existence, rather by devout sentiments, and submission to the lights of faith, than by studied reasonings and elaborate meditations" (4C, 18, p. 189).

He began with what he knew. He entered the monastery with simple faith in God's love, and over and again he told himself how loving God is. Out of the depths of a living experience he revealed the kind of life about which the poet Keats longed: "O for a life of sensations rather than thoughts!"

Some might complain that Brother Lawrence was not a trained theologian. He did not intend to be. Nor is it necessary for us to be trained in theology. Yet, in one sense he was a theologian, and so are we all. For he wrote and spoke of what he knew, a most personal faith. Knowing what he did, he acted upon it: he loved. Knowing God, he loved him. Knowing God, he loved others. Of this there never was any doubt in the mind of Brother Lawrence.

A truly great theologian of a recent generation, John Baillie of Scotland, wrote pointedly of the same thing: "However difficult it is to know what to believe, there is always something which we know beyond all doubt to be worth doing. Everywhere in the New Testament faith is a possession, not of the sharp-witted and clear-headed, but of the truehearted and the loyal."

Jesus was like that. He never asked what one believed. In his final appearance to his disciples as recorded in John 21, he did not ask Simon Peter what he believed. He asked: "Simon, son of John, do you love me?" Brother Lawrence was not bothered by theological questions and arguments. He knew enough to put what he knew into practice. He loved.

Then he wanted to know more, because he wanted to love God more. Yet he was not sure for four long years that God loved him sufficiently to save him, to forgive him his sins. Nevertheless he entered the religious life *only* out of love for God, as he told his friend: "Whatever becomes of me, whether I be lost or saved, I will always continue to act purely for the love of God. . . . That this trouble of mind had lasted four years, during which time he had suffered much; . . . but that God still continued to bestow [his favors] in abundance" (2C, 2, p. 183).

Brother Lawrence was not one with God. Brother Lawrence was man, the created; God was the creator. Yet in a real sense Brother Lawrence knew himself to be one with God in the same way that Jesus prayed that we might be one as he was one with the Holy Father. Because he did *know,* he could *love.* Evelyn Underhill illustrates this thought vividly:

We know a thing only by uniting with it; by assimilating it; by an interpenetration of it and ourselves. It gives itself to us, just in so far as we give ourselves to it; and it is because our outflow towards things is usually so perfunctory and so languid, that our comprehension of things is so perfunctory and languid too. . . . The great Sufi who said that "Pilgrimage to the place of the wise, is to escape the flame of separation" spoke the literal truth. Wisdom is the fruit of communion; ignorance the inevitable portion of those who "keep themselves to themselves" and stand apart, judging, analyzing the things which they have never truly known.

Because he has surrendered himself to it, "united" with it, the patriot knows his country, the artist knows the subject of his art, the lover his beloved, the saint his God, in a manner which is inconceivable as well as unattainable by the looker-on. Real knowledge, since it always implies an intuitive sympathy more or less intense, is far more accurately suggested by the symbols of touch and taste than by those of hearing and sight.[1]

What this suggests for us today we will see in the next chapter.

---

[1] *Practical Mysticism* (London: J. M. Dent & Sons, 1914), p. 4.

26

The Glorious Employment
of a Christian

Though the fig tree do not blossom,
    nor fruit be on the vines,
the produce of the olive fail
    and the fields yield no food,
the flock be cut off from the fold
    and there be no herd in the stalls,
yet I will rejoice in the Lord,
    I will joy in the God of my salvation. (Hab. 3:17-18.)

If any man's will is to do his will, he shall know whether the teaching is from God or whether I am speaking on my own authority. (John 7:17.)

Whether he is a sinner, I do not know; one thing I know, that though I was blind, now I see. (John 9:25.)

This is eternal life, that they know thee the only true God, and Jesus Christ whom thou has sent. (John 17:3.)

For it is the God who said, "Let light shine out of darkness," who has shone in our hearts to give the light of the knowledge of the glory of God in the face of Christ. (II Cor. 4:6.)

It is no longer I who live, but Christ who lives in me. (Gal. 2:20.)

Remember, I pray you, what I have often recommended, which is, to think often on God, by day, by night, in your business, and

152

*even in your diversions. He is always near you and with you;
leave Him not alone. You would think it rude to leave a friend
alone who came to visit you; why, then, must God be neglected?
Do not, then forget Him, but think on Him often, adore Him continually, live and die with Him; this is the glorious employment of
a Christian. In a word, this is our profession; if we do not know
it, we must learn it. (11L, 3, pp. 202-3.)*

An unknown writer prayed: "Thou before whom all imagin-
ing staggers and is felled, at whose dark boundaries comprehension can only bow in helplessness and surrender; help us
to remember that we can never know thee until we love thee
above all else." [1]

The glorious employment of a Christian, according to
Brother Lawrence, is the loving of God above all else. "Live
and die with Him." It is Paul writing to Galatia: "I live; yet
not I, but Christ liveth in me" (Gal. 2:20 KJV). Knowing
God *has* become loving him. Loving God *is* knowing him.

First, we begin with what we do know. In our homes we
come to know love through our parents and later through our
friends. If we do find love there, surrounding us, undergirding
us, it is much easier to believe that God, too, the Eternal
Father, loves us. Someone has said that "the Christian faith is
primarily concerned with the experience of relatedness, love,
acceptance, and power in our lives that transcends our common
humanity and makes life possible." When we begin to see this,
even in a small way, within the family, we may be ready to
recognize it at work elsewhere.

Think of a pair of honeymooners. Each wishes to know
everything about the other, though neither ever can know in
full the other. Yet each wishes to know more, so as to love more.
For a time romantic idealism colors the vision, but later, as the

[1] Gerald Heard, ed., *Prayers and Meditations* (New York: Harper &
Brothers, 1949), p. 27.

couple grows in true love, each sees the partner without that
coloring. Each learns to accept the other just as he is, to love
him just as he is, to live with him just as he is. Real love is always acceptance, transcending what otherwise might be a
rather commonplace home.

With God, too, we need to accept him as at times he seems
to be, not very loving, not very just, not very friendly and open.
Job, Jeremiah, and Habakkuk were three who argued with
God, not liking what they thought they found, yet continuing
to love him because of what they did know about him. Then they
were able to "live and die with Him."

So the seeker discovers what little within himself he may
know, then shares with others who too have found within
themselves the beginning of true knowledge and love. As he
continues his "glorious employment," he will find a teacher, a
book, a minister, a friend, sometimes a stranger passing by, who
will open a new window toward the "light of the knowledge
of the glory of God in the face of Christ."

Second, we must question what we see and learn, arguing
with it, studying it, doubting it, testing it. Brother Lawrence
did not do this, but most of us need to. It is part of our growing,
our searching. Unless the questions of the mind can be met—
and not necessarily answered—with honesty, there will be no
growing.

Often in prayer classes someone will complain: I can't believe
that or that doesn't make sense to me. Everything one reads
is not to be taken as gospel truth, just because it appears in a
book, even this book! One's reading should be examined, questioned, argued with, but it should not end there. That would be
fruitless. Rather, one should go on to ask: Just what is the
author trying to say? Why is he saying it? In other words,
sympathetic understanding must come before there can be in-
telligent agreement or disagreement.

Never should we be afraid of the mind. If God does not speak
to and through the mind, then he is too small. How foolish

are those who wonder if God is large enough, now that we are exploring outer space. Perhaps a greater God is out there! God is God, no small one limited to this small world we know. If our God is only that, he is indeed too small.

Brother Lawrence started with the mystery of a tree in the winter—cold, bleak, dead in appearance, yet full of life to be revealed when spring came again. Others, Job especially, have found a wonder and mystery in God revealed in nature, even though theological arguments up to that time could not resolve their questionings. Helen was shaken by a liberal approach to theology as found in a book and in discussion about it with her minister. She could not find an inner quiet. Then late one night she saw the beauty and majesty of the northern lights streaking across the heavens. Like Job she stood in awe, knowing that her mind was not yet satisfied, but that her heart was. She knew, with Keats, the meaning of his sentence, as quoted earlier, "O for a life of sensation rather than thoughts."

So Brother Lawrence acted on what he knew, impressing "deeply upon his heart the Divine existence, rather by devout sentiments, and submission to the lights of faith." This he could accept; this he could live by, limited though it might be.

Third, we will find suddenly, and in the most unexpected ways, that God reveals himself in love. John Wesley for many years puzzled over his "condition"; then his heart was strangely warmed. Before him Luther, and long before him Augustine and many others through the centuries, after months and even years of intellectual agony, found within themselves not answers, but the Answer.

No longer, then, was there need to argue. To use the mind, yes; to know as much as one could know of all the basic questions of life. But not to question God. For God is. There can be no fooling of the self then. His presence is real, more real than the evidence of the five senses, as we found in the writings of John Baillie in Chapter 4. This is the same Scottish theologian whose words were quoted in the preceding chapter:

"Everywhere in the New Testament faith is a possession, not of the sharp-witted and clear-headed, but of the true-hearted and the loyal."

This is what it means to go beyond the intellect, beyond factual knowledge. Still there will be the searching to know, to question, to understand, but this is a different searching, a searching to be aware of inwardly, in the deep consciousness. There in that inner depth we will come to know with an assurance like that of Jesus: "If any man's will is to do his will, he shall know whether the teaching is from God or whether I am speaking on my own authority."

Life will be completely changed in that knowing. It cannot be proved to others, and often it cannot be shared with others. Yet we will know.

And how? Because, in the fourth place, there will be a constant awareness of presence, a constant wonder of love. In spite of sickness and tragedy, touching both herself and her family, Ruth spoke of the greatness of God, of the wonder of his love. Talking with him constantly with "the little lifting up of the heart," a conversation quite one-sided in her adoration of him, Ruth discovered a relationship she had not known was possible.

She could not keep it to herself. She had to tell others, to reach out to others in love. Brother Lawrence did the same thing. In serving his brothers in the monastery, in writing to many, in conversations with those who came to see him, he served as God gave him opportunity. A sense of presence, if it is real, cannot be cuddled with in a chimney corner.

Robert Raynolds found this in what he called "a small parish of love."

An ordinary man, in the course of an ordinary life, builds up what amounts to a small parish of love, the good and normal congregation of those he loves and whose love he accepts, the living and the remembered, which would easily, almost any time he stopped to think about it, run into a hundred or more welcome indwellers in his heart. This is no abstract concept such as loving mankind, which so often goes with being unable to get along with your neighbor; it is not using the tricks of psychology to influence or dominate people; it is no gathering in of persons to a man's purpose; it is simply the community of persons that rises about a man during his life as a result of his having chosen to love and to accept the love offered to him. The purpose was to love, and one of the results of that choice and purpose, fulfilled with patience, courage, and humility, is just such a small parish of welcome indwellers in his heart. To know, to cherish, and to deepen the truth of living our life in the midst of this small parish of our own heart is the work of the wisdom of love.

There is a timeless place of warmth and kindness in my heart where I am thankful for each one I love and for each one who loves me; it is where each one I love is welcome; it is where God finds me when I have the courage to let Him in; it is the small parish of love, where my life is hallowed.[2]

This is the knowing that is at the heart of the sense of presence. It is the glorious employment of a Christian.

[2] *The Choice to Love* (New York: Harper & Brothers, 1959), pp. 120-21.

27

An Act
of the Will

But as for me and my house, we will serve the Lord.
(Josh. 24:15.)

A man had two sons; and he went to the first and said, "Son, go and work in the vineyard today." And he answered, "I will not"; but afterwards he repented and went. And he went to the second and said the same; and he answered, "I go, sir," but did not go. Which of the two did the will of his father? (Matt. 21:28-31.)

When the days drew near for him to be received up, he set his face to go to Jerusalem. (Luke 9:51.)

I can will what is right, but I cannot do it. For I do not do the good I want, but the evil I do not want is what I do. Now if I do what I do not want, it is no longer I that do it, but sin which dwells within me. . . . Wretched man that I am! Who will deliver me from this body of death? (Rom. 7:18-20, 24.)

Therefore take the whole armor of God, that you may be able to withstand in the evil day, and having done all, to stand. (Eph. 6:13.)

That we ought to make a great difference between the acts of the understanding and those of the will; that the first were comparatively of little value, and the others, all. That our only business was to love and delight ourselves in God. (2C, 17, pp. 184-85.)

*That all things are possible to him who **believes**; that they are less difficult to him who **hopes**; that they are more easy to him who **loves**, and still more easy to him who perseveres in the practice of these three virtues. (4C, 13, p. 188.)*

He knows what we can do. Let us begin, then. (5L, 2, p. 196.)

Our mind is extremely roving; but, as the will is mistress of all our faculties, she must recall them, and carry them to God as their last end. (9L, 1, p. 200.)

In one of his cartoons J. R. Williams pictured fifty years ago a boy standing in the doorway of his home. His mother was hurrying him. "Get along to Sunday School," she was saying, "so you'll know how to be good." His answer was brief: "I already know how to be good. That isn't my trouble."

We are just like him today. We know enough to be good. That isn't the trouble. Doing it—there lies the rub. We are brothers of the man characterized by the phrase, "Big talk, little do."

No wonder Brother Lawrence pointed out the "great difference between the acts of the understanding and those of the will." How true in the long run that the first are of comparatively little value. We know enough. We just don't act on what we know.

Paul faced this dilemma, wretched man that he was. He did not do the good he wanted to do; no, he did the evil he did not want to do. As Moffatt has translated, "The wish is there, but not the power of doing what is right."

A dentist visiting from Scotland with others of a team of Buchmanites from the British Isles sat next to Dr. John Baillie at dinner. The theologian, then professor at Union Seminary in New York, asked the dentist how Buchmanism had helped him. "God stopped me from smoking," he replied.

"You mean God said you should stop smoking?"

"Oh no," the dentist said. "I have a heart condition. My

doctor told me I should stop. But I couldn't. Then through the Oxford Group I found the power to stop."

So Brother Lawrence said many years ago. "He knows what we can do. Let us begin, then." And we too know what we can do. Why, then, don't we do it? Why do we not have the power to do what is right? What is the cause of our paralysis? If "the will is mistress of all our faculties," why does it not take charge?

When Yogi Berra was a young catcher with the New York Yankees, in one game he hit the ball safely into right field. He just shuffled along, so that he was held to one base, though he should have made two. The next batter forced Yogi at second. Then came a fly ball, followed by a third out. No run was scored. One of his teammates asked Yogi if he were feeling all right. "Yes, I feel fine," the catcher replied. "Then why didn't you run out the hit and reach second? You could have moved on to third with the next play, then scored on the fly. If you're going to be a Yankee, you must play like one." Yogi never forgot that reprimand. From then on he played with the enthusiasm of a "take-charge" player, his will being stronger than his apathy.

John Ciardi, poetry editor of *Saturday Review,* spoke one time of the men and women who constantly produce fine writing. Some fellow writers alibi, he said, that one must be a genius to write so consistently well. Not so, Ciardi continued; the truth is that those complainers seek any kind of excuse to stop writing, not "feeling" like writing, or not being in the proper mood, while the others keep on regardless of what might happen. Their persistence, as much as their narrative ability, makes them great writers. They work regularly, persistently, until they finish, regardless of mood.

In a prayer retreat a woman complained that she just could not keep to a regular time for her personal devotions. She would take time every day for a week or two; then she would miss several days or a week. "What is the answer to this?" she asked. Her retreat leader said quickly, "Do it."

For several hours she thought about this, then came back to the group. "That *is* the answer, isn't it?" she said. "Just plain, simple 'Do it!' That's all it takes!" Sometime later she reported that she no longer had trouble finding or taking time. She just did it, remembering what she had been told. "Do it" was the catalyst at the time to send her on her way, with the will taking over.

Why, then, do we hesitate to act? For one thing, we really do not wish to act. We read devotional books, we attend retreats or conferences, we talk with ministers and lay folk who have "what we want"; but we do not become involved. We want someone to tell us what to do. But to do it, to give ourselves in surrender, to set apart time for personal daily devotion, to offer ourselves as a teacher or a worker—no. We want the gifts of God without paying the price. Dr. L. was the minister of a fine church, but he thought his people needed a deepening of their spiritual life as he did. So he invited a young minister to speak about spiritual renewal through personal groups. He was thrilled, and those who heard the presentation were thrilled. Later, though, he told a neighbor, "I'd give anything to have groups like that, except—." The "except" stopped him. He really did not wish to have them. They would take time from the things he now was enjoying doing. So none was started.

Or again, many are stopped from acting because they will not give up a sin. For many months Mrs. T. prayed that her husband would stop his drinking and that she would be led to "bring him to Christ." All the time, though, she was skirting the edge of adultery with a married man. "I just can't let him go," she cried.

Several times in marriage counseling I have found similar conditions where the sinful acts or desires of one or both parties kept them from reconciliation. Sometimes these desires are not admitted. Mrs. M. for three years wrestled with what she thought was a deep religious problem. At the end of the time she discovered she was in love with a neighbor, though she had thought she "merely" liked him. When her love was recognized and rightly dealt with, her "religious problem" disappeared.

Brother Lawrence knew human nature. He knew his own weakness and that of others. Though his actions sometimes bothered him, still "he had no qualms; for, said he, when I *fail* in my duty, I readily acknowledge it, saying, *I am used to do so; I shall never do otherwise if I am left to myself.* If I fail not, then I give God thanks, acknowledging that the strength comes from Him" (2C, 20, p. 185).

His strength *did* come from God, for he found that his only business, truly, was to love and delight himself in God. Hence, "in his trouble of mind he had consulted nobody, but knowing only by the light of faith that God was present, he contented himself with directing all his actions to Him, *i.e.,* doing them with a desire to please Him, let what would come of it" (2C, 13, p. 184).

Let us too begin, then, no matter what may come of it. For this we can know with Brother Lawrence that God is present in our acts.

28

When Distractions Come

> Yet the righteous holds to his way,
>   and he that has clean hands
>   grows stronger and stronger. (Job 17:9.)

> I have gone astray like a lost sheep; seek thy servant,
>   for I do not forget thy commandments. (Ps. 119:176.)

> For thus said the Lord God, the Holy One of Israel,
>   "In returning and rest you shall be saved;
>   in quietness and in trust shall be your strength." (Isa. 30:15.)

Therefore, my beloved brethren, be steadfast, immovable, always abounding in the work of the Lord, knowing that in the Lord your labor is not in vain. (I Cor. 15:58.)

And I take captive every thought and make it obey Christ. (II Cor. 10:5 Goodspeed.)

If sometimes my thoughts wander from it by necessity or infirmity, I am soon recalled by inward emotions so charming and delightful that I am confused to mention them. (6L, 11, p. 198.)

You tell me nothing new; you are not the only one that is troubled with wandering thoughts. Our mind is extremely roving; but, as the will is mistress of all our faculties, she must recall them, and carry them to God as their last end.
    When the mind, for lack of discipline when first we engaged in

163

*devotion, has contracted certain bad habits of wandering and dis-
sipation, such habits are difficult to overcome, and commonly draw
us, even against our wills, to things of the earth.*

*I believe one remedy for this is to confess our faults and to
humble ourselves before God. I do not advise you to use multiplicity of words in prayer; many words and long discourses being
often the occasions of wandering. Hold yourself in prayer before
God like a poor, dumb, paralytic beggar at a rich man's gate. Let
it be **your business** to keep your mind in **the Presence of the
Lord.** If it sometimes wanders and withdraws itself from Him,
do not much disquiet yourself for that: trouble and disquiet serve
rather to distract the mind than to recall it; the will must bring it
back in tranquillity. If you persevere with your whole strength,
God will have pity on you.*

*One way to recall the mind easily in the time of prayer, and
preserve it more in tranquillity, is **not to let it wander too far at
other times.** You should keep it strictly in **the Presence of
God;** and being accustomed to think of Him often, you will find
it easy to keep your mind calm in the time of prayer, or at least
to recall it from its wanderings. (9L, 1-4, pp. 200-201.)*

Sometimes the will is paralyzed by distractions. We just
cannot do what we want to do because the mind refuses to hold
to one thought. It wanders all around Robin Hood's barn.

This is nothing new, of course, as Brother Lawrence was
quick to point out to his friend: "You are not the only one
that is troubled with wandering thoughts." Even today, one or
the other of two reasons upsets our prayer and meditation. We
are either like Linus, sitting against a tree in the cartoon strip,
"Peanuts," who complained, "I'm a lousy meditator. . . . I
always fall asleep"; or, like a rudderless craft in a windstorm.
This latter is our concern in this chapter.

First, said Brother Lawrence, let us "confess our faults
and . . . humble ourselves before God." We find it difficult to
concentrate. Admit it. Recognize that for most of us our minds
normally do wander. Few of us are trained to hold to one
thought very long. But then, God uses what we have; and when

our minds wander, he yet "speaks" to us through those wanderings.

Nevertheless, do not "use multiplicity of words in prayer," Brother Lawrence suggested. Simplicity of speech is an expression of simplicity of heart. To talk all around a subject in one's praying describes just what happens. We talk all around it, instead of going to the heart of it. We should toss out darts of longing, of loving, of adoration, of praise. For it is the inner desire, rather than the spoken word, that God hears.

Further, keep your prayer and meditation rather specific. To pray for people in general reveals a lack of true interest. As Linus said in another "Peanuts" cartoon, "People don't bother me. Persons do." Generalities are a form of escape. The love of God, for example, is too great a theme for meditation. Break it down into smaller topics which our simple minds can handle —the love of God seen in a parent, in a friend, in Jesus of Nazareth, in Paul's thirteenth chapter of I Corinthians, in a child's innocence, in a reformed sinner. Choose brief sentences, short phrases, even single words, and pay attention to these, looking at them from various angles.

Then again, when the mind does begin to wander, come back to that brief phrase, that central theme. Do not force this, saying, "I will hold to this even if it kills me," for it probably will kill the meditation. Emphasis, then, will be on doing it, and what one is doing will be lost. After all, a meditation is only a means to an end, the end being the sense of presence. Do as Brother Lawrence did, who was "soon recalled by inward emotions so charming and delightful that I am confused to mention them."

"A poor, dumb, paralytic beggar at a rich man's gate" will not lose himself in philosophical and theological musings. He will cry for help. It is this recognition of dependence upon God, the power and providence of an Infinite Being, that Brother Lawrence was writing about. So we should cry out for help by letting it be our business to keep our minds in the presence of

God "in praising, adoring, and loving Him unceasingly, for His infinite goodness and perfection" (4C, 3, p. 187).

This avoids the disquieting of the self against which Brother Lawrence wrote. To punish oneself, to condemn oneself as a needless wanderer, only calls attention to the wandering. Look at the new thought that has entered the mind. Instead of fighting it, welcome it, "speak" to it, bring it into the prayer of meditation, then go on with the phrase or sentence or thought to which it was alien. For example, a women's prayer class was disturbed by the pounding of brickworkers in a neighboring room. The men were tearing down a thick mortar wall, opening an entrance into a new educational building. "How can we pray with all the noise?" they queried. When they remembered that the noise was necessary if they were to have new children's rooms, then they thanked God for the workmen—and almost immediately forgot the noise!

A veterinarian faced a similar problem. "How do you think of God," Dr. K. wanted to know, "when a cow steps on your foot?" Later he found an answer. He could either say "God damn you" and be damned, or "God bless you" and be blessed. He learned to say "God bless you" and discovered that a sore foot need not take him away from God.

Finally, though, Brother Lawrence offered a sound piece of advice. How should I keep my mind from wandering in time of prayer? Do not "let it wander too far at other times"! A scatterbrain generally is a scatterbrain in prayer. Inability to "center down" in one's normal thought will cause a similar inability during the time of prayer. This Kierkegaard knew with his phrase, "purity of heart is to will one will." Not occasionally, not when the interest is caught, but all the time. Again it is Jesus saying, "You cannot serve God and mammon."

Once again we return to a major emphasis of the monastery cook: be disciplined through habit, making the will the mistress of all our faculties. "We must, nevertheless, always work at it, for, in the spiritual life, not to advance is to go back."

29

When Suffering
Comes

I consider that the sufferings of this present time are not worth comparing with the glory that is to be revealed to us. (Rom. 8:18.)

But we have this treasure in earthen vessels, to show that the transcendent power belongs to God and not to us. We are afflicted in every way, but not crushed; perplexed, but not driven to despair; persecuted, but not forsaken; struck down, but not destroyed; always carrying in the body the death of Jesus, so that the life of Jesus may also be manifested in our bodies. . . .

So we do not lose heart. Though our outer nature is wasting away, our inner nature is being renewed every day. For this slight momentary affliction is preparing for us an eternal weight of glory beyond all comparison. (II Cor. 4:7-10, 16-17.)

For I will show him how much he must suffer for the sake of my name. (Acts 9:16.)

Five times I have received at the hands of the Jews the forty lashes less one. Three times I have been beaten with rods; once I was stoned. Three times I have been shipwrecked; a night and a day I have been adrift at sea; on frequent journeys, in danger from rivers, danger from robbers, danger from my own people, danger from Gentiles, danger in the city, danger in the wilderness, danger at sea, danger from false brethren; in toil and hardship, through many a sleepless night, in hunger and thirst, often without food, in cold and exposure. And, apart from other things, there is the daily pressure upon me of my anxiety

for all the churches. Who is weak, and I am not weak? Who is made
to fall, and I am not indignant? (II Cor. 11:24-29.)

*That he expected, after the pleasant days God had given him, he
should have his turn of pain and suffering; but that he was not
uneasy about it, knowing very well that as he could do nothing
of himself, God would not fail to give him the strength to bear it.*
(2C, 4, p. 183.)

*I know not what God purposes with me, or keeps me for; I am in a
calm so great that I fear nought. What can I fear, when I am with
Him? And with Him, in his Presence, I hold myself the most I can.*
(7L, 3, p. 199.)

*I do not pray that you may be delivered from your troubles, but I
pray God earnestly that He would give you strength and patience
to bear them as long as He pleases. . . .*

   *I wish you could convince yourself that God is often nearer
to us, and more effectually present with us, in sickness than in
health. Rely upon no other physician; for, according to my apprehension, He reserves your cure to Himself. Put, then, all your
trust in Him, and you will soon find the effects of it in your recovery, which we often retard by putting greater confidence in
medicine than in God.*

   *Whatever remedies you make use of, they will succeed only
so far as He permits. When pains come from God, He alone can
cure them. He often sends diseases on the body to cure those of
the soul. Comfort yourself with the sovereign physician both of
the soul and body. (12L, 1-3, p. 203.)*

*If we were well accustomed to the exercise of the **Presence** of
God, all bodily diseases would be much alleviated thereby. God
often permits that we should suffer a little to purify our souls and
oblige us to continue **with Him.** I cannot understand how a soul,
which is with God and which desires Him alone, can feel pain:
I have had enough experience to banish all doubt that it can.*

   *Take courage; offer Him your pains unceasingly; pray to Him
for strength to endure them. Above all, acquire a habit of conversing often with God, and forget Him the least you can. Adore
Him in your infirmities, offer yourself to Him from time to time,*

*and in the very height of your sufferings beseech Him humbly
and affectionately (as a child his good father) to grant you the
aid of His grace and to make you conformable to His holy will.
(13L, 1-2, p. 204.)*

*I am in pain to see you suffer so long. What gives me some ease
and sweetens the sorrow I have for your griefs is that I am convinced that they are tokens of God's love for you. Look at them in
this light and you will bear them more easily. As your case is, it is
my opinion that you should leave off human remedies, and resign
yourself entirely to the providence of God. Perhaps He stays only
for that resignation and a perfect trust in Him to cure you. Since,
notwithstanding all your cares, medicine has hitherto proved unsuccessful, and your malady still increases, it will not be tempting
God to abandon yourself into His hands and expect all from Him.*

*I told you in my last that He sometimes permits the body to
suffer to cure the sickness of the soul. Have courage, then; make
a virtue of necessity. Ask of God, not deliverance from the body's
pains, but strength to bear resolutely, for the love of Him, all that
He should please, and as long as He shall desire.*

*Such prayers, indeed, are a little hard to nature, but most ac-
ceptable to God, and sweet to those that love Him. Love sweetens
pain; and when one loves God, one suffers for His sake with joy
and courage. Do you so, I beseech you; comfort yourself with
Him, who is the only physician of all our ills. He is the Father of
the afflicted, always ready to help us. He loves us infinitely, more
than we imagine. Love Him, then, and seek no other relief than in
Him. (14L, 1-3, p. 205.)*

Has any generation ever been so fascinated with its own
physical health as this one? The host of new drugs and patent
medicines creates fortunes for their discoverers or manufac-
turers surpassed only perhaps by the advertisers who make
their appeal to our fear of pain and suffering. With the increasing longevity of life, the advent of Medicare, and the
growth both in number and size of hospitals and nursing
homes, there is a dearth both of doctors and nurses, even though

more are practicing than ever before. Yet with all this there still is no remedy for the old hill woman who asked the missionary: "Do you have any medicine for fear?"

In Brother Lawrence's time medical care was quite primitive. Doctors were little more than leeches. Drugs were superstitious folk medicines on the whole. Yet sickness and suffering, perhaps because they were so prevalent, were not the bane of man's days as they are now.

Nevertheless, then as well as now, people hurried to "spiritual" healers, miracle workers, quacks, witch doctors, and careful practitioners, hoping against hope that somehow their pains might be lessened, their illnesses healed. Today more and more churches are holding healing services with a variety of programs. Let a revivalist announce a healing ministry, and crowds flock to him. In retreats and conferences where various seminars are offered, those which deal with intercession (almost wholly concerned with sickness) or spiritual healing have the bulk of enrollees. Our bodies often demand more attention than our souls!

Brother Lawrence put the attention back where it belonged. He brought a maturing faith to his friends which we need rather desperately in our own time.

First, he was thoroughly realistic. He would not fool himself, and he would not fool others. Sooner or later pain and suffering would come to him, he knew, as it must come to all. Why, then, be uneasy about it? Within himself he could do nothing about it, but God could. Did that mean God would take it away, keep old age from coming, destroy all sickness and suffering? Brother Lawrence was not so foolish as to believe that. God would do what he alone could do, give the sufferer strength to endure.

In his realism, he helped his friend face her seemingly incurable condition. She had tried doctors, and their medicine no longer helped. Brother Lawrence would not turn from them— to do so would be tempting God—rather, he would "make a

virtue of necessity." Evidently all that the doctors could do had
been done; now it was up to the providence of God. Hence,
he suggested that she should turn now from doctors and their
remedies, and let her trust lie wholly in God. Not that he would
cure her. Yet Brother Lawrence did understand that her struggling to find a cure might well be a barrier to God's healing
power.

Her prayers, then, should not be for deliverance from pain,
but for strength to endure. How difficult to pray like that!
He admitted so himself, for they are "a little hard to nature";
yet God is "the Father of the afflicted, always ready to help
us." A maturing faith will resign itself to endure when one is
in the condition of his friend and there is no other recourse.

Second, in addition to his realism and actually a part of it,
is his sound advice to accept one's condition and to endure it.
This is no "weak resignation," no cowed denial of life. It is an
understanding of life, an acceptance of reality. Pain will come
sooner or later. Suffering will fall upon all of us before too long.
To deny it, to fight it, to try to hide from it, will only make the
pain and suffering worse.

Instead, we should know that God will give us strength
through his grace by which we may endure, being able to take
whatever may come. For the moment the suffering is what God
permits—not that he wants it or deliberately sends it. Brother
Lawrence did hint that it came from God, for he wrote, "They
consider sickness as a pain of nature, and not as from God;
and seeing it only in that light, they find nothing in it but grief
and distress. But those who consider sickness as coming from
the hand of God, as the effect of His mercy, and the means
which He employs for their salvation—such commonly find in
it great consolation" (12L, 1, p. 203).

His belief that nothing happened outside the knowledge and
love of God helped Brother Lawrence accept whatever came.
After all, he had found in his own experience that God "often
sends diseases of the body to cure those of the soul." He had

found that physical infirmity quickly brings one to a new understanding of his dependence upon God.

If we had the perspective of God's love, how much easier it
would be to accept what comes. We are finite. We cannot know.
But we can ask for strength and patience to bear what comes.

This accepting we alone can do. Others may give us medicines or may pray for us or otherwise may tend us in our ill-
ness. We alone can accept with strength and patience what
comes. We alone can "adore Him in [our] infirmities, offer
[ourselves] to Him from time to time, and in the very height
of [our] sufferings beseech Him humbly and affectionately
. . . to grant . . . the aid of His grace" (13L, 2, p. 204).

Third, when this aid comes, there will be revealed the fruit
of a relationship that Brother Lawrence had not heard about
by name, but knew well by experience, the relationship of psy-
chosomatic medicine. Knowing that he would be unable to do
anything about possible sickness to himself, he was not uneasy
about it. His refusal to be upset or to be overly anxious in itself
helped him to overcome his sickness later. To his friend in a
later letter, he told of his own experience. "I have been often
near expiring, but I never was so much satisfied as then. Accordingly, I did not pray for any relief, but I prayed for
strength to suffer with courage, humility, and love." (15L, 1,
p. 206.)

In this he revealed the true power of prayer. It is not a magic
or superstition that moves or changes God. It is the way in
which one sees himself in the light of God's perspective, through
which one brings himself under obedience to God. Instead of
trying to manipulate God, true prayer helps man become a par-
ticipant in God's will for him. Hence, Brother Lawrence found
a "calm so great that I fear nought. What can I fear, when I
am with Him?"

So certain was he of the interrelationship between the emotions and the physical body that he wrote: "If we were well
accustomed to the exercise of *the Presence of God,* all bodily

diseases would be much alleviated thereby." He even went so far as to wonder how anyone who is truly with God and desirous of him alone could feel pain. But his realism broke through when he wrote further: "I have had enough experience to banish all doubt that it can"! His own pain, in spite of his constant sense of presence, told him that. He *knew* that having a continual sense of the presence of God well might go along with intense suffering.

Many have found even as he did that "love sweetens pain." Then how much easier it is to suffer for his sake with the joy and courage both of Brother Lawrence and of the apostle Paul.

Fourth, we see Brother Lawrence's maturing faith in his belief that through everything that happened ran the thread of God's love. His high notion of God did not desert him in time of pain and suffering. "Comfort yourself with Him, who is the only Physician of all our ills," he tells us today just as he wrote to his friend some three hundred years ago. For God "loves us infinitely, more than we imagine."

Along with Brother Lawrence many of us have discovered that "God is often nearer to us, and more effectually present with us, in sickness than in health." Then it is that we see our human condition, that we recognize as seldom before our dependence upon him for life. Not that we will then grovel before him. Not at all. We are his children. When we do put all our trust in him, we often find the effects of it in our recovery. And when this is not certain, something else is: "They are tokens of God's love." So he wrote: "Look at them in this light and you will bear them more easily." Hence, we too must "ask of God, not deliverance from the body's pains, but strength to bear resolutely, for the love of Him, all that He should please, and as long as He shall desire."

This demands a maturing faith. Brother Lawrence had it. So can we.

30

A Continual Walk with God

The earth produces of itself, first the blade, then the ear, then the full grain in the ear. (Mark 4:28.)

Be patient, therefore, brethren, until the coming of the Lord. Behold, the farmer waits for the precious fruit of the earth, being patient over it until it receives the early and the late rain. You also be patient. (James 5:7-8.)

To those who by patience in well-doing seek for glory and honor and immortality, he will give eternal life. (Rom. 2:7.)

To you has been given the secret of the kingdom of God, but for those outside everything is in parables; so that they may indeed see but not perceive, and may indeed hear but not understand. (Mark. 4:11-12.)

She seems to me full of good will, but she wants to go faster than grace. One does not become holy all at once. (10L, 1, p. 201.)

That all bodily mortifications and other exercises are useless, except as they serve to arrive at the union with God by love; that he had well considered this, and found it the shortest way to go straight to Him by a continual practice of love and doing all things for His sake. . . .
That all possible kinds of mortification, if they were devoid of the love of God, could not efface a single sin. That we ought without anxiety to expect the pardon of our sins from the blood of

174

Jesus Christ, laboring simply to love Him with all our hearts. That God seemed to have granted the greatest favors to the greatest sinners, as more signal monuments of His mercy. (2C, 16, 18, pp. 184-85.)

That in the beginning of the spiritual life we ought to be faithful in doing our duty and denying ourselves; but after that, unspeakable pleasures followed. That in difficulties we need only have recourse to Jesus Christ and beg His grace; with that everything became easy.

That many do not advance in the Christian progress because they stick in penances and particular exercises, while they neglect the love of God, which is the end. (3C, 9, 10, p. 186.)

I do not say that therefore we must put any violent constraint upon ourselves. No, we must serve God in a holy freedom; we must do our business faithfully, without trouble or disquiet, recalling our mind to God meekly, and with tranquillity, as often as we find it wandering from Him. (4L, 4, p. 195.)

There is not in the world a kind of life more sweet and delightful than that of a continual walk with God. Those only can comprehend it who practise and experience it; yet I do not advise you to do it from that motive. It is not pleasure which we ought to seek in this exercise; but let us do it from the motive of love, and because God would have us so walk.

*Were I a preacher, I should, above all other things, preach **the practice of the Presence of God**; and were I a "director," I should advise all the world to do it, so necessary do I think **it**, and so easy, too.*

*Ah! knew we but the need we have of the grace and assistance of God, we should never lose sight of Him—no, not for a moment. Believe me; this very instant, make a holy and firm resolution nevermore wilfully to stray from Him, and to live the rest of your days **in His sacred Presence,** for love of Him surrendering, if He think fit, all other pleasures. (3L, 3-5, p. 194.)*

Have you found for yourself this "sacred Presence"? As you have experimented with these exercises, have you come into "a

continual walk with God"? Or have you read these pages only
for their possible intellectual or devotional content? If the last
has been your motive, you have wasted your time.

Brother Lawrence as much as told M. Beaufort this at the
end of their first conversation. Come again, the monastery cook
said, if you seek sincerely to serve God; otherwise, just stay
away. No need to waste the time of either of us.

Anyway, just to read about it, just to hear about it, will do
little good. After all, only those who practice it, who experience
it within themselves, will know what it really is.

Some, though, may be disappointed. How faint is that sense!
Surely by this time one should "have arrived." After these
days and weeks of meditation and practice, especially when one
brings eager searching along with his desire, one's experiments
ought to have brought greater satisfaction. God should have revealed himself by now.

Of a young woman like that Brother Lawrence wrote aptly:
"She seems to me full of good will, but she wants to go faster
than grace. One does not become holy at once." This we forget.
So fine will be the end result of our searching that we want it
now—or sooner! Why does God hold off granting to us his
presence? Nothing would be more pleasurable to us.

That may be our difficulty. It is God's gifts we seek, the
pleasure (and perhaps the power) that will come to us, rather
than God himself. It is a motive of selfishness, the joy, the
wonder, the delight, the strength that we may have for ourselves.

Certainly, though, there is nothing wrong in seeking these,
is there? Of course not. But consider how the earth bears
fruit: "first the blade, then the ear, then the full grain in the
ear." Spiritual growth is similar. No one is a full-blown saint
overnight. Consider the apostle Paul. Most people believe he
became a Christian missionary within weeks of his Damascus
experience. Actually, either fourteen or seventeen years passed
between his conversion and his call through Barnabas to be a

missionary (see Galatians 1:18–2:1). He spent those long
years in Tarsus, preparing himself for whatever might come.
He waited for grace to move when he, Paul, was ready for it.

Francis de Sales, whose *Introduction to a Devout Life* is one
of the finest treatises on the spiritual life, compared the healing
of spirit with that of the body.

The ordinary purification, or healing, whether of the body or the
mind, is not instantaneously effected, but takes place gradually,
by passing from one degree to another, with labor and patience.

The angels upon Jacob's ladder had wings, yet they flew not, but
ascended and descended in order from one step to another. The
soul that rises from sin to devotion may be compared to the dawning
of the day, which at its approach expels not the darkness instantaneously, but by little and little. "The cure," says the medical
aphorism, "which is made leisurely, is always the most perfect."
The diseases of the heart, as well as those of the body, come posting
on horseback, but depart leisurely on foot. Courage and patience
then, Philothea, are necessary in this enterprise.

Yes, some are disappointed that they cannot move faster
than grace. Others, though, less ready to give up, believe that
penances will hurry their "sainthood." The body supposedly is
the source of all evil; hence, put it under heavy discipline, even
punishment. Few today, of course, wear hair shirts or the like,
yet through fastings of food, of sleep, of sexual relationships,
some would "mortify the flesh." Or they would abandon certain pleasures, such as theatergoing, card playing, mixed swim-
ming and what not, making certain thereby that the spirit, they
think, will conquer the flesh.

These practices are valueless, wrote Brother Lawrence, unless
the love of God goes along with them. In themselves mortifications "could not efface a single sin." Only the love of God
does this. So, having found this to be true during the early
years of his monastery life, he "found it the shortest way to go
straight to Him by a continual practice of love and doing all

things for His sake." If it seems wise to God that certain pleasures later should be surrendered, all right. Otherwise, pay no attention to such denials.

From his own experience he knew that God showed great mercy to great sinners, just as Paul knew that to the chief of all sinners had come God's love. Regret, yes, that was there. "I am filled with shame and confusion when I reflect, on one hand, upon the great favors which God has bestowed and is still bestowing upon me; and, on the other, upon the ill use I have made of them, and my small advancement in the way of perfection" (10L, 2, p. 201). Along with Paul, "forgetting what lies behind and straining forward to what lies ahead," he pressed on to the goal of his "sacred Presence."

He was without "any violent constraint," though, even in this. We must strive for a "holy freedom," not troubling ourselves with questionings and probings and self-condemnatory lashings of the mind; we must accept "the grace and assistance of God" as it is offered to us.

When we can do this, then indeed, "There is not in the world a kind of life more sweet and delightful than that of a continual walk with God."

Have you found this to be true in your own life? Are you as certain as Brother Lawrence that "God would have us so walk"? If not, then you cannot comprehend it, for only those who practice and experience it, as he said, will know. In that same seventeenth century Benjamin Whichcote, an English Quaker, said: "If you say you have a revelation from God, I must have a revelation from God too before I can believe you." But if it is your revelation too, continually to practice the presence of God, then you "should advise all the world to do it, so necessary [will you] think it, and so easy too."

Brother Lawrence

His Conversations and Letters on the
Practice of the Presence of God

From the Preface to the Original
French Edition, A.D. 1692

"Although death has carried off last year many of the Order of the Carmelites Dechausses, brethren who have left in dying rare legacies of lives of virtue; Providence, it would seem, has desired that the eyes of men should be cast chiefly on Brother Lawrence . . .

"Several persons having seen a copy of one of his letters, have desired to see more; and to meet this wish, care has been taken to collect as many as possible of those which Brother Lawrence wrote with his own hand . . .

"All Christians will find herein much that is edifying. Those in the thick of the great world will learn from these letters how greatly they deceive themselves, seeking for peace and joy in the false glitter of the things that are seen, yet temporal: those who are seeking the Highest Good will gain from this book strength to persevere in the practice of virtue. All, whatever their lifework, will find profit, for they will see herein a brother, busied as they are in outward affairs, who in the midst of the most exacting occupations, has learnt so well to accord action with contemplation, that for the space of more than forty years he hardly ever turned from the Presence of God."

Conversations

First Conversation

August 3, 1666

1. THE first time I saw Brother Lawrence was upon the third of August, 1666. He told me that God had done him a singular favor, in his conversion at the age of eighteen.

2. That in the winter, seeing a tree stripped of its leaves, and considering that within a little time the leaves would be renewed, and after that the flowers and fruit appear, he received a high view of the providence and power of God, which has never since been effaced from his soul. That this view had perfectly set him loose from the world, and kindled in him such a love for God that he could not tell whether it had increased during the more than forty years he had lived since.

3. That he had been footman to M. Fieubert, the treasurer, and that he was a great awkward fellow who broke everything.

4. That he had desired to be received into a monastery, thinking that he would there be made to smart for his awkwardness and the faults he should commit, and so he should sacrifice to God his life, with its pleasures; but that God had disappointed him, he having met with nothing but satisfaction in that state.

5. That we should establish in ourselves a sense of God's Presence by continually conversing with Him. That it was a shameful thing to quit His conversation to think of trifles and fooleries.

6. That we should feed and nourish our souls with high notions of God, which would yield us great joy in being devoted to Him.

7. That we ought to *quicken—i.e., to enliven—our faith.* That it was lamentable we had so little; and that instead of taking *faith* for the rule of their conduct, men amused themselves with trivial devotions which changed daily. That the way of faith was the spirit of the Church, and that it was sufficient to bring us to a high degree of perfection.

8. That we ought to give ourselves up entirely to God, with regard both to things temporal and spiritual, and seek our satisfaction only in the fulfilling of His will, whether He lead us by suffering or by consolation, for all would be equal to a soul truly resigned. That there was need of fidelity in those times of dryness, or insensibility and irksomeness in prayer, by which God tries our love to Him; that *then* was the time for us to make good and effectual acts of resignation, whereof one alone would oftentimes very much promote our spiritual advancement.

9. That as for the miseries and sins he heard of daily in the world, he was so far from wondering at them that, on the contrary, he was surprised that there were not more, considering the malice sinners were capable of; that, for his part, he prayed for them; but knowing that God could remedy the mischiefs they did, when He pleased, he gave himself no further trouble.

10. That to arrive at such resignation as God requires, we should watch attentively over all the passions which mingle as well in spiritual things as in those of a grosser nature; that God would give light concerning those passions to those who truly desire to serve Him. That if this was my design, *viz.*, sincerely to serve God, I might come to him (Brother Lawrence) as often as I pleased, without any fear of being troublesome; but if not, that I ought no more to visit him.

Second Conversation

September 28, 1666

1. That he had always been governed by love, without selfish views; and that having resolved to make the love of God the *end* of all his actions, he had found good reason to be well satisfied with his method. That he was pleased when he could take up a straw from the ground for the love of God, seeking Him only, and nothing else, not even His gifts.

2. That he had been long troubled in mind from a sure belief that he was lost; that all the men in the world could not have persuaded him to the contrary; but that he had thus reasoned with himself about it: *I engaged in a religious life only for the love of God, and I have endeavored to act only for Him; whatever becomes of me, whether I be lost or saved, I will always continue to act purely for the love of God. I shall have this good at least, that till death I shall have done all that is in me to love Him.* That this trouble of mind had lasted four years, during which time he had suffered much; but that at last he had seen that this trouble arose from want of faith, and that since then he had passed his life in perfect liberty and continual joy. That he had placed his sins betwixt him and God, as it were to tell Him that he did not deserve His favors, but that God still continued to bestow them in abundance.

3. That in order to form a habit of conversing with God continually, and referring all we do to Him, we must at first apply to Him with some diligence; but that after a little care we should find His love inwardly excite us to it without any difficulty.

4. That he expected, after the pleasant days God had given him, he should have his turn of pain and suffering; but that he was not uneasy about it, knowing very well that as he could do nothing of himself, God would not fail to give him the strength to bear it.

5. That when an occasion of practising some virtue offered, he addressed himself to God, saying, *Lord, I cannot do this unless Thou enablest me;* and that then he received strength more than sufficient.

6. That when he had failed in his duty, he simply confessed his fault, saying to God, *I shall never do otherwise if Thou leavest me to myself; it is Thou who must hinder my falling, and mend what is amiss.* That after this he gave himself no further uneasiness about it.

7. That we ought to act with God in the greatest simplicity, speaking to Him frankly and plainly, and imploring His assistance in our affairs just as they happen. That God never failed to grant it, as he had often experienced.

8. That he had been lately sent into Burgundy to buy the provision of wine for the Society, which was a very unwelcome task to him, because he had no turn for business, and because he was lame and could not go about the boat but by rolling himself over the casks. That, however, he gave himself no uneasiness about it, nor about the purchase of the wine. That he said to God, *It was His business he was about,* and that afterwards he found it very well performed. That he had been sent into Auvergne the year before upon the same account;

that he could not tell how the matter passed, but that it proved very well.

9. So, likewise, in his business in the kitchen (to which he had naturally a great aversion), having accustomed himself to do everything there for the love of God, and with prayer, upon all occasions, for His grace to do his work well, he had found everything easy during the fifteen years that he had been employed there.

10. That he was very well pleased with the post he was now in; but that he was as ready to quit that as the former, since he was always finding pleasure in every condition by doing little things for the love of God.

11. That with him the *set* times of prayer were not different from other times; that he retired to pray, according to the directions of his Superior, but that he did not want such retirement, nor ask for it, because his greatest business did not divert him from God.

12. That as he knew his obligation to love God in all things, and as he endeavored so to do, he had no need of a *director* to advise him, but that he needed much a *confessor* to absolve him. That he was very very sensible of his faults, but not discouraged by them; that he confessed them to God, but did not plead against Him to excuse them. When he had so done, he peaceably resumed his usual practice of love and adoration.

13. That in his trouble of mind he had consulted nobody, but knowing only by the light of faith that God was present, he contented himself with directing all his actions to Him, *i.e.,* doing them with a desire to please Him, let what would come of it.

14. That useless thoughts spoil all; that the mischief began there, but that we ought to reject them as soon as we perceived their impertinence to the matter in hand or to our salvation, and return to our communion with God.

15. That at the beginning he had often passed his time appointed for prayer in rejecting wandering thoughts and falling back into them. That he could never regulate his devotion by certain methods as some do. That, nevertheless, at first he had *meditated* for some time, but afterwards that went off in a manner he could give no account of.

16. That all bodily mortifications and other exercises are useless, except as they serve to arrive at the union with God by love; that he had well considered this, and found it the shortest way to go straight to Him by a continual practice of love and doing all things for His sake.

17. That we ought to make a great difference between the acts of the *understanding* and those of the *will;* that the first were comparatively of little value, and the others, all. That our only business was to love and delight ourselves in God.

18. That all possible kinds of mortification, if they were devoid of the love of God, could not efface a single sin. That we ought without anxiety to expect the pardon of our sins from the blood of Jesus Christ, laboring simply to love Him with all our hearts. That God seemed to have granted the greatest favors to the greatest sinners, as more signal monuments of His mercy.

19. That the greatest pains or pleasures of this world were not to be compared with what he had experienced of both kinds in a spiritual state; so that he was careful for nothing and feared nothing, desiring only one thing of God, *viz.,* that he might not offend Him.

20. That he had no qualms; for, said he, when I *fail* in my duty, I readily acknowledge it, saying, *I am used to do so; I shall never do otherwise if I am left to myself.* If I fail not, then I give God thanks, acknowledging that the strength comes from Him.

Third Conversation

November 22, 1666

1. He told me that the *foundation of the spiritual life* in *him* had been a high notion and esteem of God in faith; which when he had once well conceived, he had no other care but faithfully to reject at once every other thought, *that he might perform all his actions for the love of God.* That when sometimes he had not thought of God for a good while, he did not disquiet himself for it; but after having acknowledged his wretchedness to God, he returned to Him with so much the greater trust in Him as he had found himself wretched through forgetting Him.

2. That the trust we put in God honors Him much and draws down great graces.

3. That it was impossible not only that God should deceive, but also that He should long let a soul suffer which is perfectly surrendered to Him, and resolved to endure everything for His sake.

4. That he had so often experienced the ready succor of Divine Grace upon all occasions, that from the same experience, when he had business to do, he did not think of it beforehand; but when it was time to do it, he found in God, as in a clear mirror, all that was fit for him to do. That of late he had acted thus, without anticipating care; but before the experience above mentioned, he had been full of care and anxiety in his affairs.

5. That he had no recollection of what things he had done, once they were past, and hardly realized them when he was about them: that on leaving table, he knew not what he had been eating; but that with one single end in view, he did all for the love of God, rendering Him thanks for that He had directed these acts, and an infinity of others throughout his life: he did all very simply, in a manner which kept him ever stead-fastly in the loving Presence of God.

6. When outward business diverted him a little from the thought of God, a fresh remembrance coming from God, invested his soul, and so inflamed and transported him that it was difficult for him to restrain himself.

7. That he was more united to God in his ordinary occupations than when he left them for devotion in retirement, from which he knew himself to issue with much dryness of spirit.

8. That he expected hereafter some great pain of body or mind; that the worst that could happen to him would be to lose that sense of God which he had enjoyed so long; but that the goodness of God assured him that He would not forsake him utterly, and that He would give him strength to bear whatever evil He permitted to happen to him; and therefore that he feared nothing, and had no occasion to con-sult with anybody about his soul. That when he had attempted to do it, he had always come away more perplexed; and that as he was conscious of his readiness to lay down his life for the love of God, he had no apprehension of danger. That perfect abandonment to God was the sure way to heaven, a way on which we had always sufficient light for our conduct.

9. That in the beginning of the spiritual life we ought to be faith-ful in doing our duty and denying ourselves; but after that, unspeakable pleasures followed. That in difficulties we need only have recourse to Jesus Christ and beg His grace; with that everything became easy.

10. That many do not advance in the Christian progress because they stick in penances and particular exercises, while they neglect the love of God, which is the *end*. That this appeared plainly by their works, and was the reason why we see so little solid virtue.

11. That there was need neither of art nor science for going to God, but only a heart resolutely determined to apply itself to nothing but Him, or for *His* sake, and to love Him only.

Fourth Conversation

November 25, 1667

1. He discoursed with me very fervently and with great openness of heart, concerning his manner of *going to God,* whereof some part is related already.

2. He told me that all consists *in one hearty renunciation* of everything which does not lead us to God in order that we may accustom ourselves to a continual conversation with Him, with freedom and in simplicity. That we need only to recognize God intimately present with us, and to address ourselves to Him every moment, that we may beg His assistance for knowing His will in things doubtful, and for rightly performing those which we plainly see He requires of us; offering them to Him before we do them, and giving Him thanks when we have done.

3. That in this conversation with God we are also employed in praising, adoring, and loving Him unceasingly, for His infinite goodness and perfection.

4. That without being discouraged on account of our sins, we should pray for His grace with perfect confidence, relying upon the infinite merits of our Lord Jesus Christ. That God never failed to offer us His grace at every action; that he distinctly perceived it, and never failed of it, unless when his thoughts had wandered from a sense of God's Presence, or he had forgotten to ask His assistance.

5. That God always gave us light in our doubts when we had no other design but to please Him, and to act for His love.

6. That our sanctification did not depend upon *changing* our works, but in doing that for God's sake which commonly we do for our own. That it was lamentable to see how many people mistook the means for the end, addicting themselves to certain works, which they performed very imperfectly, by reason of their human or selfish regards.

7. That the most excellent method he had found of going to God was that of *doing our common business* without any view of pleasing men,* and (as far as we are capable) *purely for the love of God.*

8. That it was a great delusion to think that the times of prayer ought to differ from other times; that we are as strictly obliged to adhere to God by action in the time of action as by prayer in the season of prayer.

9. That his view of prayer was nothing else but a sense of the

* Galatians i. 10; Ephesians vi. 5, 6.

Presence of God, his soul being at that time insensible to everything but Divine Love; and that when the appointed times of prayer were past, he found no difference, because he still continued with God, praising and blessing Him with all his might, so that he passed his life in continual joy; yet hoped that God would give him somewhat to suffer when he should have grown stronger.

10. That we ought, once for all, heartily to put our whole trust in God, and make a full surrender of ourselves to Him, secure that He would not deceive us.

11. That we ought not to be weary of doing little things for the love of God, who regards not the greatness of the work, but the love with which it is performed. That we should not wonder if, in the beginning, we often failed in our endeavors, but that at last we should gain a habit, which will naturally produce its acts in us, without our care, and to our exceeding great delight.

12. That the whole substance of religion was faith, hope, and love, by the practice of which we become united to the will of God; that all besides is indifferent, and to be used only as a means that we may arrive at our end, and be swallowed up therein, by faith and love.

13. That all things are possible to him who *believes;* that they are less difficult to him who *hopes;* that they are more easy to him who *loves,* and still more easy to him who perseveres in the practice of these three virtues.

14. That the end we ought to propose to ourselves is to become, in this life, the most perfect worshippers of God we can possibly be, as we hope to be through all eternity.

15. That when we enter upon the spiritual life, we should consider and examine to the bottom what we are. And then we should find ourselves worthy of all contempt, and not deserving indeed the name of Christians; subject to all kinds of misery and numberless accidents, which trouble us and cause perpetual vicissitudes in our health, in our humors, in our internal and external dispositions; in short, persons whom God would humble by many pains and labors, within as well as without. After this we should not wonder that troubles, temptations, oppositions, and contradictions happen to us from men. We ought, on the contrary, to submit ourselves to them, and bear them as long as God pleases, as things highly beneficial to us.

16. That the greater perfection a soul aspires after, the more dependent it is upon Divine Grace.

17. * Being questioned by one of his own Society (to whom he

---

* The particulars which follow are collected from other accounts of Brother Lawrence.

was obliged to open himself) by what means he had attained such an habitual sense of God, he told him that, since his first coming to the monastery, he had considered God as the *end* of all his thoughts and desires, as the mark to which they should tend, and in which they should terminate.

18. That in the beginning of his novitiate he spent the hours appointed for private prayer in thinking of God, so as to convince his mind of, and to impress deeply upon his heart, the Divine existence, rather by devout sentiments, and submission to the lights of faith, than by studied reasonings and elaborate meditations. That by this short and sure method he exercised himself in the knowledge and love of God, resolving to use his utmost endeavor to live in a continual sense of His Presence, and, if possible, never to forget Him more.

19. That when he had thus in prayer filled his mind with great sentiments of that Infinite Being, he went to his work appointed in the kitchen (for he was cook to the Society). There having first considered severally the things his office required, and when and how each thing was to be done, he spent all the intervals of his time, as well before as after his work, in prayer.

20. That when he began his business, he said to God, with a filial trust in Him: *O my God, since Thou art with me, and I must now, in obedience to Thy commands, apply my mind to these outward things, I beseech Thee to grant me the grace to continue in Thy Presence; and to this end do Thou prosper me with Thy assistance, receive all my works, and possess all my affections.*

21. ["We can do *little* things for God. I turn the cake that is frying on the pan for love of Him, and that done, if there is nothing else to call me, I prostrate myself in worship before Him, who has given me grace to work; afterwards I rise happier than a king. It is enough for me to pick up but a straw from the ground for the love of God."]

22. As he proceeded in his work he continued his familiar conversation with his Maker, imploring His grace, and offering to Him all his actions.

23. When he had finished he examined himself how he had discharged his duty; if he found *well*, he returned thanks to God; if otherwise, he asked pardon; and without being discouraged, he set his mind right again, and continued his exercise of the *Presence of God,* as if he had never deviated from it. "Thus," said he, "by rising after my falls, and by frequently renewed acts of faith and love, I am come to a state wherein it would be as difficult for me not to think of God as it was at first to accustom myself to it."

24. As Brother Lawrence had found such comfort and blessing in walking in the Presence of God, it was natural for him to recommend it earnestly to others; but his example was a stronger inducement than any arguments he could propose. His very countenance was edifying; such a sweet and calm devotion appearing in it as could not but affect all beholders. And it was observed that in the greatest hurry of business in the kitchen, he still preserved his recollection and heavenly-mindedness. He was never hasty nor loitering, but did each thing in its season, with an even, uninterrupted composure and tranquillity of spirit. "The time of business," said he, "does not with me differ from the time of prayer, and in the noise and clatter of my kitchen, while several persons are at the same time calling for different things, I possess God in as great tranquillity as if I were upon my knees at the Blessed Sacrament."

Letters

First Letter

1. *My Reverend Mother:* Since you desire so earnestly that I should communicate to you the method by which I arrived at that *habitual sense of God's Presence,* which our Lord, of His mercy, has been pleased to vouchsafe to me, I must tell you that it is with great difficulty that I am prevailed on by your importunities; and now I do it only upon the terms that you show my letter to nobody. If I knew that you would let it be seen, all the desire that I have for your perfection would not be able to determine me to it.

2. The account I can give you is this.

3. Having found in many books different methods of going to God, and divers practices of the spiritual life, I thought this would serve rather to puzzle me than facilitate what I sought after, which was nothing else than how to become wholly God's. This made me resolve to give the *all* for the *all;* so after having given myself wholly to God, to make all the satisfaction I could for my sins, *I renounced, for the love of Him, everything that was not His, and I began to live as if there was none but He and I in the world.* Sometimes I considered myself before Him as a poor criminal at the feet of his judge; at other times I beheld Him in my heart as my Father, as my God. I worshipped Him the oftenest that I could, keeping my mind in His holy Presence, and recalling it as often as I found it wandering from Him. I found no small trouble in this exercise, and yet I continued it, notwithstanding all the difficulties that I encountered, without troubling or disquieting myself when my mind had wandered involuntarily. I made this my business as much all the day long as at the appointed times of prayer; for at all times, every hour, every minute, even in the height of my business, I drove away from my mind everything that was capable of interrupting my thought of God.

4. Such has been my common practice ever since I entered monastic life; and though I have done it very imperfectly, yet I have found great advantages by it. These, I well know, are to be imputed solely to the mercy and goodness of God, because we can do nothing without Him, and *I* still less than any. But when we are faithful to keep ourselves in His holy Presence, and set Him always before us, this not only hinders our offending Him and doing anything that may displease Him, at least wilfully, but it also begets in us a holy freedom, and, if I may so speak, a familiarity with God, wherewith we ask, and that successfully, the graces we stand in need of. In short, by often repeating these acts, they become *habitual,* and the *Presence of God* is rendered as it were *natural* to us. Give Him thanks, if you please, with me, for His great goodness toward me, which I can never sufficiently marvel at, for the many favors He has done to so miserable a sinner as I am. May all things praise Him. Amen.

I am, in our Lord, Yours, ——

Second Letter

1. *My Reverend Mother:* I have taken this opportunity to communicate to you the thoughts of one of our Society, concerning the wonderful effect and continual succor which he receives from *the Presence of God.* Let you and me both profit by them.

2. You must know that during the forty years and more that he has spent in religion, his continual care has been to be *always with God;* and to do nothing, say nothing, and think nothing which may displease Him, and this without any other view than purely for the love of Him, and because He deserves infinitely more.

3. He is now so accustomed to that *Divine Presence* that he receives from it continual succor upon all occasions. For above thirty years his soul has been filled with joys so continual, and sometimes to transcendent, that he is forced to use means to moderate them, and to prevent their appearing outwardly.

4. If sometimes he is a little too much absent from the *Divine Presence,* which happens often when he is most engaged in his outward

business, God presently makes Himself felt in his soul to recall him. He answers with exact fidelity to these inward drawings, either by an elevation of his heart toward God, or by a meek and loving regard to Him; or by such words as love forms upon these occasions, as for instance, *My God, behold me, wholly Thine: Lord, make me according to Thy heart.* And then it seems to him (as in effect he feels it) that this God of love, satisfied with such few words, reposes again, and rests in the depth and center of his soul. The experience of these things gives him such an assurance that God is always deep within his soul, that no doubt of it can arise, whatever may betide.

5. Judge from this what contentment and satisfaction he enjoys, feeling continually within him so great a treasure. No longer is he in anxious search after it, but he has it open before him, free to take of it what he pleases.

6. He complains much of our blindness, and exclaims often that we are to be pitied who content ourselves with so little. *God's treasure,* he says, *is like an infinite ocean, yet a little wave of feeling, passing with the moment, contents us. Blind as we are, we hinder God and stop the current of His graces. But when He finds a soul permeated with a living faith, He pours into it His graces and favors plenteously; into the soul they flow like a torrent which, after being forcibly stopped against its ordinary course, when it has found a passage, spreads with impetuosity its pent-up flood.*

7. Yes, we often stop this torrent by the little value we set upon it. But let us stop it no longer; let us enter into ourselves and break down the barrier which holds it back. Let us make the most of the day of grace; let us redeem the time that is lost, for perhaps we have but little left. Death follows us close; let us be well prepared for it; for we die but once, and a miscarriage *then* is irretrievable.

8. I say again, let us enter into ourselves. Time presses, there is no room for delay; our souls are at stake. You, I believe, have taken such effectual measures that you will not be surprised. I commend you for it; it is the one thing needful. We must, nevertheless, always work at it, for, in the spiritual life, not to advance is to go back. But those whose spirits are stirred by the breath of the Holy Spirit go forward even in sleep. If the vessel of our soul is still tossed with winds and storms, let us awake the Lord, who reposes in it, and He will quickly calm the sea.

9. I have taken the liberty to impart to you these good thoughts, that you may compare them with your own. It will serve again to rekindle and inflame them, if by misfortune (which God forbid, for it would be

indeed a great misfortune) they should be, though never so little, cooled. Let us then *both* recall our early fervor. Let us profit by the example and thoughts of this brother, who is little known of the world, but known of God, and abundantly blessed by Him. I will pray for you; do you pray instantly for me. I am, in our Lord,   Yours,———
June 1, 1682

Third Letter

1. *My Reverend and Greatly Honored Mother:* I have received today two books and a letter from Sister ———, who is preparing to make her "profession," and upon that account desires the prayers of your holy Community, and yours in particular. I perceive that she reckons much upon them; pray do not disappoint her. Beg of God that she may make her sacrifice in the view of His love alone, and with firm resolution to be wholly devoted to Him. I will send you one of these books, which treat of *the Presence of God,* a subject which in my opinion contains the whole spiritual life; and it seems to me that whoever duly practises it will soon become spiritual.

2. I know that for the right practice of it the heart must be empty of all else, because God wills to possess the heart *alone;* and as He cannot possess it *alone* unless it be empty of all besides, so He cannot work in it what He would, unless it be left vacant to Him.

3. There is not in the world a kind of life more sweet and delightful than that of a continual walk with God. Those only can comprehend it who practise and experience it; yet I do not advise you to do it from that motive. It is not pleasure which we ought to seek in this exercise; but let us do it from the motive of love, and because God would have us so walk.

4. Were I a preacher, I should, above all other things, preach *the practice of the Presence of God;* and were I a "director," I should advise all the world to do it, so necessary do I think it, and so easy, too.

5. Ah! knew we but the need we have of the grace and assistance of God, we should never lose sight of Him—no, not for a moment. Believe me; this very instant, make a holy and firm resolution nevermore wilfully to stray from Him, and to live the rest of your days *in His sacred Presence,* for love of Him surrendering, if He think fit, all other pleasures.

6. Set heartily about this work, and if you perform it as you ought, be assured that you will soon find the effects of it. I will assist you with my prayers, poor as they are. I commend myself earnestly to yours and those of your holy Community, being theirs, and more particularly

Yours,———

1685

Fourth Letter

1. *To the Same:* I have received from Mdlle. ——— the things which you gave her for me. I wonder that you have not given me your thoughts on the little book I sent to you, and which you must have received. Pray, set heartily about the practice of it in your old age; it is better late than never.

2. I cannot imagine how religious persons can live satisfied without *the practice of the Presence of God*. For my part, I keep myself retired with Him in the very center of my soul as much as I can; and while I am so with Him I fear nothing, but the least turning away from Him is to me insupportable.

3. This exercise does not much fatigue the body; yet it is proper to deprive it sometimes, nay often, of many little pleasures which are innocent and lawful, for God will not permit that a soul which desires to be devoted entirely to Him should take other pleasures than with Him: that is more than reasonable.

4. I do not say that therefore we must put any violent constraint upon ourselves. No, we must serve God in a holy freedom; we must do our business faithfully, without trouble or disquiet, recalling our mind to God meekly, and with tranquillity, as often as we find it wandering from Him.

5. It is, however, necessary to put our whole trust in God, laying aside all other cares, and even some particular forms of devotion, though very good in themselves, yet such as one often engages in unreasonably, because these devotions are only means to attain to the end. So when by this *practice of the Presence of God* we are *with Him* who is *our End,* it is then useless to return to the means. Then it is that abiding in His holy Presence, we may continue our commerce of love, now by an act of adoration, of praise, or of desire; now by an act of sacrifice or of thanksgiving, and in all the manners which our mind can devise.

6. Be not discouraged by the repugnance which you may find to it from nature; you must do yourself violence. Often, at the onset, one thinks it is lost time; but you must go on, and resolve to persevere in it till death, notwithstanding all the difficulties that may occur. I commend myself to the prayers of your holy Community, and to yours in particular. I am, in our Lord, Yours,———

November 3, 1685

Fifth Letter

1. *Madame:* I pity you much. It will be of great importance if you can leave the care of your affairs to M. and Mme. ———, and spend the remainder of your life only in worshiping God. He lays no great burden upon us: a little remembrance of Him from time to time; a little adoration; sometimes to pray for His grace, sometimes to offer Him your sorrows, and sometimes to return Him thanks for the benefits He has given you, and still gives you, in the midst of your troubles. He asks you to console yourself with Him the oftenest you can. Lift up your heart to Him even at your meals and when you are in company; the least little remembrance will always be acceptable to Him. You need not cry very loud; He is nearer to us than we think.

2. To be with God, there is no need to be continually in church. We may make an oratory of our heart wherein to retire from time to time to converse with Him in meekness, humility, and love. Everyone is capable of such familiar conversation with God, some more, some less. He knows what we can do. Let us begin, then. Perhaps He is just waiting for one generous resolution on our part. Have courage. We have but little time to live; you are near sixty-four, and I am almost eighty. Let us live and die with God. Sufferings will be sweet and pleasant to us while we are with Him; and without Him, the greatest pleasures will be anguish to us. May He be blessed for all. Amen.

3. Accustom yourself, then, by degrees thus to worship Him, to beg His grace, to offer Him your heart from time to time in the midst of your business, even every moment, if you can. Do not scrupulously confine yourself to fixed rules, or particular forms of devotion, but act with faith in God, with love and humility. You may assure M. and Mme. and Mdlle. ——— of my poor prayers, and that I am their servant, and particularly

Yours in our Lord, ———

Sixth Letter

1. *My Reverend Father:* Not finding my manner of life in books, although I have no difficulty about it, yet, for greater security, I shall be glad to know your thoughts concerning it.

2. In a conversation some days since with a person of piety, he told me that the spiritual life was a life of grace, which begins with servile fear, which is increased by hope of eternal life, and which is consummated by pure love; that each of these states had its different stages, by which one arrives at last at that blessed consummation.

3. I have not followed all these methods. On the contrary, from I know not what instincts, I found that they discouraged me. This was the reason why, at my entrance into religion, I resolved to give myself up to God as the best satisfaction I could make for my sins, and for the love of Him to renounce all besides.

4. For the first years I commonly employed myself during the time set apart for devotion with the thought of death, judgment, heaven, hell, and my sins. Thus I continued some years, applying my mind carefully the rest of the day, and even in the midst of my business, *to the Presence of God,* whom I considered always as *with* me, often as *in* me.

5. At length I came insensibly to do the same thing during my set time of prayer, which caused in me great delight and consolation. This practice produced in me so high an esteem for God that *faith* alone was capable to satisfy me in that point.

6. Such was my beginning; and yet I must tell you that for the first ten years I suffered much. The apprehension that I was not devoted to God as I wished to be, my past sins always present to my mind, and the great unmerited favors which God bestowed on me, were the matter and source of my sufferings. During this time I fell often, yet as often rose again. It seemed to me that all creation, reason, and God Himself were against me, and *faith* alone for me. I was troubled sometimes with thoughts that to believe I had received such favors was an effect of my presumption, which pretended to be *at once* where others arrive only with difficulty; at other times, that it was a wilful delusion, and that there was no salvation for me.

7. When I thought of nothing but to end my days in these times of trouble and disquiet (which did not at all diminish the trust I had in God, and which served only to increase my faith), I found myself changed all at once; and my soul, which till that time was in trouble, felt a profound inward peace, as if it had found its center and place of rest.

8. Ever since that time I walk before God in simple faith, with humility and with love, and I apply myself diligently to do nothing and think nothing which may displease Him. I hope that when I have done what I can, He will do with me what He pleases.

9. As for what passes in me at present, I cannot express it. I have no pain nor any doubt as to my state, because I have no will but that of God, which I endeavor to carry out in all things, and to which I am so submissive that I would not take up a straw from the ground against His order, or from any other motive than purely that of love to Him.

10. I have quitted all forms of devotion and set prayers but those to which my state obliges me. And I make it my only business to persevere in His holy Presence, wherein I keep myself by a simple attention and an absorbing passionate regard to God, which I may call an *actual Presence of God;* or, to speak better, a silent and secret conversation of the soul with God . . .

11. If sometimes my thoughts wander from it by necessity or infirmity, I am soon recalled by inward emotions so charming and delightful that I am confused to mention them. I beg you to reflect rather upon my great wretchedness, of which you are fully informed, than upon the great favors which God does me, all unworthy and ungrateful as I am.

12. As for my set hours of prayer, they are only a continuation of the same exercise. Sometimes I consider myself there as a stone before a carver, whereof he is to make a statue; presenting myself thus before God, I desire Him to form His perfect image in my soul, and make me entirely like Himself.

13. At other times, when I apply myself to prayer, I feel all my spirit and all my soul lift itself up without any trouble or effort of mine, and it remains as it were in elevation, fixed firm in God as in its center and its resting-place.

14. I know that some charge this state with inactivity, delusion, and self-love. I confess that it is a holy inactivity, and would be a happy self-love were the soul in that state capable of such; because, in fact, while the soul is in this repose, it cannot be troubled by such acts as it was formerly accustomed to, and which were then its support, but which would now rather injure than assist it.

15. Yet I cannot bear that this should be called delusion, because the soul which thus enjoys God desires herein nothing but Him. If this be delusion in me, it belongs to God to remedy it. May He do with me what He pleases; I desire only Him, and to be wholly devoted to Him. You will, however, oblige me in sending me your opinion, to

which I always pay a great deference, for I have a singular esteem for
your Reverence, and am, in our Lord, my Reverend Father,

Yours, ———

Seventh Letter

1. *My Reverend and Greatly Honored Mother:* My prayers, of little
worth though they be, will not fail you; I have promised it, and I will
keep my word. How happy we might be, if only we could find the
Treasure, of which the Gospel tells us—all else would seem to us
nothing. How infinite it is! The more one toils and searches in it, the
greater are the riches that one finds. Let us toil therefore unceasingly
in this search, and let us not grow weary and leave off, till we have
found . . .

2. I know not what I shall become: it seems to me that peace of
soul and repose of spirit descend on me, even in sleep. To be without
the sense of this peace would be affliction indeed; but with this calm
in my soul even for purgatory I would console myself.

3. I know not what God purposes with me, or keeps me for; I am
in a calm so great that I fear nought. What can I fear, when I am
with Him? And with Him, in His Presence, I hold myself the most I
can. May all things praise Him. Amen.   Yours, ———

Eighth Letter

1. *Madame:* We have a God who is infinitely gracious and knows
all our wants. I always thought that He would reduce you to ex-
tremity. He will come in His own time, and when you least expect it.
Hope in Him more than ever; thank Him with me for the favors He
does you, particularly for the fortitude and patience which He gives
you in your afflictions. It is a plain mark of the care He takes of you.
Comfort yourself, then, with Him, and give thanks for all.

2. I admire also the fortitude and bravery of M. ———. God has
given him a good disposition and a good will; but there is in him still
a little of the world and a great deal of youth. I hope the affliction
which God has sent him will prove a wholesome medicine to him, and
make him take stock of himself. It is an accident which should engage

him to put all his trust in *Him* who accompanies him everywhere. Let him think of Him as often as he can, especially in the greatest dangers. A little lifting up of the heart suffices. A little remembrance of God, one act of inward worship, though upon a march and sword in hand, are prayers which, however short, are nevertheless very acceptable to God; and far from lessening a soldier's courage in occasions of danger, they best serve to fortify it.

3. Let him think then of God the most he can. Let him accustom himself, by degrees, to this small but holy exercise. No one will notice it, and nothing is easier than to repeat often in the day these little acts of inward worship. Recommend to him, if you please, that he think of God the most he can, in the manner here directed. It is very fit and most necessary for a soldier, who is daily in danger of his life, and often of his salvation. I hope that God will assist him and all the family, to whom I present my service, being theirs and in particular

Yours, ———

October 12, 1688

Ninth Letter

(*Concerning Wandering Thoughts in Prayer*)

1. *My Reverend and Greatly Honored Mother:* You tell me nothing new; you are not the only one that is troubled with wandering thoughts. Our mind is extremely roving; but, as the will is mistress of all our faculties, she must recall them, and carry them to God as their last End.

2. When the mind, for lack of discipline when first we engaged in devotion, has contracted certain bad habits of wandering and dissipation, such habits are difficult to overcome, and commonly draw us, even against our wills, to things of the earth.

3. I believe one remedy for this is to confess our faults and to humble ourselves before God. I do not advise you to use multiplicity of words in prayer; many words and long discourses being often the occasions of wandering. Hold yourself in prayer before God like a poor, dumb, paralytic beggar at a rich man's gate. Let it be *your business* to keep your mind in *the Presence of the Lord.* If it sometimes wanders and withdraws itself from Him, do not much disquiet yourself for that: trouble and disquiet serve rather to distract the mind than to recall it;

the will must bring it back in tranquillity. If you persevere with your whole strength, God will have pity on you.

4. One way to recall the mind easily in the time of prayer, and preserve it more in tranquillity, is *not to let it wander too far at other times.* You should keep it strictly in *the Presence of God;* and being accustomed to think of Him often, you will find it easy to keep your mind calm in the time of prayer, or at least to recall it from its wanderings.

5. I have told you already at large, in my former letters, of the advantages we may draw from this *practice of the Presence of God.* Let us set about it seriously, and pray for one another.

Yours, ———

Tenth Letter

1. *To the Same:* The inclosed is an answer to that which I received from our good Sister ———; pray deliver it to her. She seems to me full of good will, but she wants to go faster than grace. One does not become holy all at once. I commend her to you; we ought to help one another by our advice, and still more by our good examples. You will oblige me by letting me hear of her from time to time, and whether she be very fervent and very obedient.

2. Let us thus think often that our only business in this life is to please God, and that all besides is perhaps but folly and vanity. You and I have lived a monastic life more than forty years. Have we employed those years in loving and serving God, who by His mercy has called us to this state, and for that very end? I am filled with shame and confusion when I reflect, on one hand, upon the great favors which God has bestowed and is still bestowing upon me; and, on the other, upon the ill use I have made of them, and my small advancement in the way of perfection.

3. Since by His mercy He gives us still a little time, let us begin in earnest; let us repair the lost time; let us return with a wholehearted trust to that *Father of mercies,* who is always ready to receive us into His loving arms. Let us renounce and renounce generously, with single heart, for the love of Him, all that is not His; He deserves infinitely more. Let us think of Him perpetually. Let us put all our trust in Him. I doubt not but that we shall soon find the effects of it in receiving the abundance of His grace, with which we can do all things, and without which we can do nothing but sin.

4. We cannot escape the dangers which abound in life without the actual and *continual* help of God. Let us, then, pray to Him for it *continually*. How can we pray to Him without being with Him? How can we be with Him but in thinking of Him often? And how can we often think of Him unless by a holy habit of thought which we should form? You will tell me that I am always saying the same thing. It is true, for this is the best and easiest method I know; and as I use no other, I advise all the world to do it. We must *know* before we can *love*. In order to *know* God, we must often *think* of Him; and when we come to *love* Him, we shall then also think of Him often, for our heart will be with our treasure. This is an argument which well deserves your consideration.   I am, Yours, ———
March 28, 1689

Eleventh Letter

1. *Madame:* I have had a good deal of difficulty to bring myself to write to M. ———, and I do it now purely because you and Mme. ——— desire me. Pray write the directions and send it to him. I am very well pleased with the trust which you have in God; I wish that He may increase it in you more and more. We cannot have too much confidence in so good and faithful a Friend, who will never fail us in this world or the next.

2. If M. ——— knows how to profit by the loss he has had, and puts all his confidence in God, He will soon give him another friend, more powerful and more inclined to serve him. He disposes of hearts as He pleases. Perhaps M. ——— was too much attached to him he has lost. We ought to love our friends, but without encroaching upon our chief love which is due to God.

3. Remember, I pray you, what I have often recommended, which is, to think often on God, by day, by night, in your business, and even in your diversions. He is always near you and with you; leave Him not alone. You would think it rude to leave a friend alone who came to visit you; why, then, must God be neglected? Do not, then, forget Him, but think on Him often, adore Him continually, live and die with Him; this is the glorious employment of a Christian. In a word, this is our

profession; if we do not know it, we must learn it. I will endeavor to
help you with my prayers, and am, in our Lord,   Yours, ――――
October 29, 1689

Twelfth Letter

1. *My Reverend and Greatly Honored Mother:* I do not pray that
you may be delivered from your troubles, but I pray God earnestly that
He would give you strength and patience to bear them as long as He
pleases. Comfort yourself with Him who holds you fastened to the
cross. He will loose you when He thinks fit. Happy those who suffer
with Him. Accustom yourself to suffer in that manner, and seek from
Him the strength to endure as much and as long as He shall judge
to be necessary for you. The men of the world do not comprehend
these truths, nor is it to be wondered at, since they suffer as lovers
of the world, and not as lovers of Christ. They consider sickness as a
pain of nature, and not as from God; and seeing it only in that light,
they find nothing in it but grief and distress. But those who consider
sickness as coming from the hand of God, as the effect of His mercy,
and the means which He employs for their salvation—such commonly
find in it great consolation.

2. I wish you could convince yourself that God is often nearer to
us, and more effectually present with us, in sickness than in health. Rely
upon no other physician; for, according to my apprehension, He reserves your cure to Himself. Put, then, all your trust in Him, and you
will soon find the effects of it in your recovery, which we often retard
by putting greater confidence in medicine than in God.

3. Whatever remedies you make use of, they will succeed only so
far as He permits. When pains come from God, He alone can cure
them. He often sends diseases of the body to cure those of the soul.
Comfort yourself with the sovereign Physician both of the soul and
body.

4. I foresee that you will tell me that I am very much at my ease,
that I eat and drink at the table of the Lord. You are right: but think
you that it would be a small pain to the greatest criminal in the world
to eat at his king's table and to be served by his king's hands, without
however being assured of pardon? I believe that he would feel exceeding
great uneasiness, and such as nothing could moderate, save only his
trust in the goodness of his sovereign. So I can assure you that what-

ever pleasures I taste at the table of my King, my sins ever present before my eyes, as well as the uncertainty of my pardon, torment me: though in truth, that torment itself is pleasing.

5. Be satisfied with the state in which God places you; however happy you may think me, I envy you. Pains and sufferings would be a paradise to me while I should suffer with my God, and the greatest pleasures would be a hell to me if I could relish them without Him. All my joy would be to suffer something for His sake.

6. I must, in a little time, go to God. What comforts me in this life is that I now see Him by *faith;* and I see Him in such a manner as might make me say sometimes, *I believe no more, but I see.* I feel what faith teaches us, and in that assurance and that practice of faith I will live and die with Him.

7. Continue, then, always with God; it is the only support and comfort for your affliction. I shall beseech Him to be with you. I present my service to the Reverend Mother Superior, and commend myself to your prayers, and am, in our Lord,   Yours, ———
November 17, 1690

Thirteenth Letter

1. *My Good Mother:* If we were well accustomed to the exercise of *the Presence of God,* all bodily diseases would be much alleviated thereby. God often permits that we should suffer a little to purify our souls and oblige us to continue *with Him.* I cannot understand how a soul, which is with God and which desires Him alone, can feel pain: I have had enough experience to banish all doubt that it can.

2. Take courage; offer Him your pains unceasingly; pray to Him for strength to endure them. Above all, acquire a habit of conversing often with God, and forget Him the least you can. Adore Him in your infirmities, offer yourself to Him from time to time, and in the very height of your sufferings beseech Him humbly and affectionately (as a child his good father) to grant you the aid of His grace and to make you conformable to His holy will. I shall endeavor to help you with my poor halting prayers.

3. God has many ways of drawing us to Himself. He sometimes hides Himself from us; but *faith* alone, which will not fail us in time of need, ought to be our support, and the foundation of our confidence, which must be all in God.

4. I know not how God will dispose of me. Happiness grows upon me. The whole world suffers; yet I, who deserve the severest discipline, feel joys so continual and so great that I can scarce contain them.

5. I would willingly ask of God a share of your sufferings, but that I know my weakness, which is so great that if He left me one moment to myself I should be the most wretched man alive. And yet I know not how He can leave me alone, because faith gives me as strong a conviction as sense can do that He never forsakes us until we have first forsaken Him. Let us fear to leave Him. Let us be always with Him. Let us live and die in His Presence. Do you pray for me as I for you.

I am, Yours, ———

November 28, 1690

Fourteenth Letter

1. *To the Same:* I am in pain to see you suffer so long. What gives me some ease and sweetens the sorrow I have for your griefs is that I am convinced that they are tokens of God's love for you. Look at them in this light and you will bear them more easily. As your case is, it is my opinion that you should leave off human remedies, and resign yourself entirely to the providence of God. Perhaps He stays only for that resignation and a perfect trust in Him to cure you. Since, notwithstanding all your cares, medicine has hitherto proved unsuccessful, and your malady still increases, it will not be tempting God to abandon yourself into His hands and expect all from Him.

2. I told you in my last that He sometimes permits the body to suffer to cure the sickness of the soul. Have courage, then; make a virtue of necessity. Ask of God, not deliverance from the body's pains, but strength to bear resolutely, for the love of Him, all that He should please, and as long as He shall desire.

3. Such prayers, indeed, are a little hard to nature, but most acceptable to God, and sweet to those that love Him. Love sweetens pain; and when one loves God, one suffers for His sake with joy and courage. Do you so, I beseech you; comfort yourself with Him, who is the only Physician of all our ills. He is the Father of the afflicted, always ready to help us. He loves us infinitely, more than we imagine. Love Him, then, and seek no other relief than in Him. I hope you will soon receive it. Adieu. I will help you with my prayers, poor as they are, and shall always be, in our Lord,   Yours, ———

Fifteenth Letter

1. *To the Same:* I render thanks to our Lord for having relieved you a little, according to your desire. I have been often near expiring, but I never was so much satisfied as then. Accordingly, I did not pray for any relief, but I prayed for strength to suffer with courage, humility, and love. Ah, how sweet it is to suffer with God! However great the sufferings may be, receive them with love. It is paradise to suffer and be with Him; so that if even now in this life we would enjoy the peace of paradise, we must accustom ourselves to a familiar, humble, affectionate conversation with Him. We must prevent our spirits' wandering from Him upon any occasion. We must make our heart a spiritual temple, wherein to adore Him unceasingly. We must watch continually over ourselves, that we may not do nor say nor think anything that may displease Him. When our minds are thus filled with God, suffering will become full of sweetness, and of quiet joy.

2. I know that to arrive at this state the beginning is very difficult, for we must act purely in faith. But though it is difficult, we know also that we can do all things with the grace of God, which He never refuses to them who ask it earnestly. Knock, keep on knocking, and I answer for it that He will open to you in His due time, and grant you all at once what He has deferred many years. Adieu. Pray to Him for me as I pray to Him for you. I hope to see Him very soon.

I am, Yours, ―――

January 22, 1691

Sixteenth Letter

1. *To the Same:* God knoweth best what is needful for us, and all that He does is for our good. If we knew how much He loves us, we should always be ready to receive equally and with indifference from His hand the sweet and the bitter. All would please that came from Him. The sorest afflictions never appear intolerable, except when we see them in the wrong light. When we see them as dispensed by the hand of God, when we know that it is our loving Father who abases and distresses us, our sufferings lose all their bitterness and our mourning becomes all joy.

2. Let all our business be to *know* God; the more one *knows* Him, the more one *desires* to know Him. And as *knowledge* is commonly the measure of *love,* the deeper and more extensive our *knowledge* shall be, the greater will be our *love;* and if our love of God be great, we shall love Him equally in grief and in joy.

3. Let us not content ourselves with loving God for the mere sensible favors, how elevated soever, which He has done or may do us. Such favors, though never so great, cannot bring us so near to Him as faith does in one simple act. Let us seek Him often by faith. He is within us; seek Him not elsewhere. If we do love Him alone, are we not rude, and do we not deserve blame, if we busy ourselves about trifles which do not please and perhaps offend Him? It is to be feared these *trifles* will one day cost us dear.

4. Let us begin to be devoted to Him in good earnest. Let us cast everything besides out of our hearts. He would possess them alone. Beg this favor of Him. If we do what we can on our parts, we shall soon see that change wrought in us which we aspire after. I cannot thank Him sufficiently for the relief He has vouchsafed you. I hope from His mercy the favor of seeing Him within a few days.* Let us pray for one another. I am, in our Lord, Yours. ———

February 6, 1691

* He took to his bed two days after, and died within the week.